Curtains and Draperies

Curtains and Draperies

Do-It-Yourself
Window
Treatments

edited by
Linda Neubauer

**Creative Publishing
international**

Chanhassen, MN

Creative Publishing
international

Copyright © 2007
Creative Publishing international
18705 Lake Drive East
Chanhassen, Minnesota 55317
1-800-328-3895
www.creativepub.com
All rights reserved

President/CEO: Ken Fund
Executive Editor: Alison Brown Cerier
Executive Managing Editor: Barbara Harold
Senior Editor: Linda Neubauer
Photo Stylist: Joanne Wawra
Creative Director: Brad Springer
Photographers: Andrea Rugg, Peter Caley
Production Manager: Laura Hokkanen
Photo Researcher: Kathleen Stoehr
Page Design and Layout: Lois Stanfield
Illustrator: Deborah Pierce

Library of Congress Cataloging-in-Publication Data

The complete photo guide to curtains and draperies : do-it-yourself window treatments / Edited by Linda Neubauer.
    p. cm.
  ISBN-13: 978-1-58923-269-3 (soft cover)
  ISBN-10: 1-58923-269-0 (soft cover)
  1. Draperies. 2. Draperies--Pictorial works. I. Neubauer, Linda. II.
Title.
  TT390.C64 2007
  646.2'1--dc22   2006021109

Printed in China
10 9 8 7 6 5 4 3 2 1

Thanks to these companies for contributing their products:
Waverly Fabrics
(800)423-5881, www.waverly.com.
decorator fabrics for how-to steps
Textol Systems, Inc.
(800) 624-8746, www.draperysupply.com
grommett tape (page 17)
Rockland Industries, Inc.
(800) 876-2566, www.roc-lon.com
drapery lining for how-to steps

Photography credits:
ADO USA, pp. 5 (top), 17 (top), 28, 44, 57 (bottom), 112; Jeff Allen, p. 23 (top), design by Donna Elle; Suzanne Blackwelder, p. 17 (bottom); Casa Fiora, p. 81 (bottom); Kathie Chrisicos, p. 16; Comfortex Window Fashions, p. 11 (top); Conso Company, p. 76; Tony Giammarino, pp. 35 (top), 45 (bottom), 62, 77 (top), 80, 99 (top), 102; Hunter Douglas Window Fashions, pp. 10, 63 (top), 63 (bottom), 103 (top); David Duncan Livingston, pp. 22, 103 (bottom), 106; Silk Trading Company, p. 41 (bottom); Stroheim & Romann, p. 98; Jessie Walker Photography, pp. 6, 7 (left), 29 (top), 35 (bottom), 50, 51 (bottom), 57 (top), 67, 71, 89 (bottom); Waverly, p. 45 (top); Linda Yackle, pp. 7, 51 (bottom); Interiors by Decorating Den, www.decoratingden.com and Greg Brown, design by Julie Meyers, p. 11 (bottom); Interiors by Decorating Den, www.decoratingden.com and D. Randolph Foulds: design by Suzanne Price, pp. 23 (bottom), 89 (top); design by Adrian Halperin, back cover (top), pp. 34, 81 (top); design by Lynne Lawson, p. 81 (top); design by Sally Giar, pp. 5 (bottom), 94; design by Connie Thompson, p. 95 (top and bottom); Interiors by Decorating Den, www.decoratingden.com and Ashley Ranson: design by Marg Anquetil, p. 29 (bottom); design by Jeanne Grier, pp. 41 (top), 113 (bottom); Interiors by Decorating Den, www.decoratingden.com and Joseph Lapeyra: design by Sharon Binkerd, pp. 8, 40; Interiors by Decorating Den, www.decoratingden.com and Stacey Bradford: design by Marisa Lupo, p. 98 (bottom); Interiors by Decorating Den, www.decoratingden.com and Doug Barnett: design by Janet White, p. 107 (top); Interiors by Decorating Den, www.decoratingden.com and Mark Burgess: design by Berrett/Jakab/Zimmerman/Cochran, p. 107 (bottom); Interiors by Decorating Den, www.decoratingden.com: design by Babara Tabak, pp. 7 (right), 88

Contents

Choosing a Style

CURTAINS AND DRAPERIES have a tremendous impact on your home's décor. Considering how much space window treatments take up, their color and pattern have as much or more influence over the decorating scheme of the room as the furnishings and artwork. The ambiance of the room is reflected in the style of the window treatment, from casual tab-top curtains to formal pinch-pleated draperies, and lots of choices in between.

In the overall decorating budget, window treatments often cost more than the furniture, especially when the treatments are custom designed. You can reduce those costs by half if you make curtains and draperies yourself. You don't need professional sewing skills to get professional results. Even though they require long expanses of fabric, some curtain styles are easily made with just straight seams and hems. Even more complex-looking pleated draperies are easy to make, following the directions and photos in this book.

Function

Consider what you want your treatments to do for the room. At the very least, they disguise the hard surfaces and angles of the windows with soft, graceful folds of fabric. Some treatments must block or screen the light that enters the room and provide privacy. These usually need to open and close by sliding back and forth on the rod. If the treatment is simply decorative, it can hang over the window, be drawn back to the side, or hang over the sides of the window frame. If the window is frequently opened and closed, choose a curtain or drapery style that gives you easy access to the window.

For most of the treatments in this book, you have the choice of making them lined or unlined. Lining gives your curtains and draperies more body and protects the fabric from sun damage. It can also prevent light from shining through the fabric and making seams more visible. Of course, if sheer or semisheer curtains are what you have in mind, they should be unlined.

Form

Like the rest of your home, your window treatments are a reflection of you and your favorite decorating style. There are curtains and draperies to match any mood and décor—casual, fun, upbeat, contemporary, trendy, classic, formal, traditional—and hundreds of possible fabrics, rods, and trims to make your curtains and draperies unique.

What length should you make your treatment? There are suggestions and examples for each style. In general, sill-length curtains are very casual, suitable for kitchens, bathroom, and bedrooms. Floor-length, breaking on the floor, or puddling on the floor are all more formal. Use these lengths for the living room, dining room, or master bedroom. If your curtains are intended to open and close, however, avoid the puddles.

How to Use This Book

HERE ARE INSTRUCTIONS for twenty different styles of curtains and draperies that you might use for your home. Some are classic styles that have stood the test of time and some are more contemporary and trendy. Photographs show each style in a variety of room settings with different fabrics, embellishments, and hardware. You'll see how decorators have approached common window shapes and locations, as well as unique arrangements and sizes.

Once you have chosen a curtain or drapery style, the step-by-step instructions will tell you how to construct it from beginning to end: measuring, cutting, sewing, and installing. It is a good idea to read all the instructions before you start. The "What you need to know" section will help with the planning; it covers information like what size to make the treatments, what types of fabric are suitable, and how and where to mount the hardware.

Also, before you start, read through the basics section beginning on page 118. Its insights and tips will help you get professional results. You may not be familiar with some of the special terms used for window treatments, so these are explained in "Terms to Know" at the back of the book. The terms appear in italics the first time they come up in a project.

Materials

Each project has a materials list of things you'll likely need to buy. The list doesn't tell you how much fabric to buy because that depends on the size of the window, the length of the treatment, and how far out to the sides of the window you want the treatment to go. The materials list assumes you already have basic sewing supplies on hand, such as pins, fabric shears, steel tape measure, carpenter's square for marking straight cutting lines, fabric marking pens or pencils, sewing machine and attachments, thread, iron, and pressing surface.

Cutting directions

Curtains and draperies are made from long lengths of fabric that are cut straight across the ends, with the length running parallel to the selvages. Often two or more widths of fabric must be sewn together. Cutting directions are set apart in each project to help you find the correct *cut length* for each piece and the total *cut width*. You simply multiply the cut length by the number of fabric widths needed to determine how much fabric to buy.

Take some time to check out all the curtain and drapery styles and then start planning your own window treatments. What a thrill it will be when you tell everyone you made them yourself!

Flat Panel Curtains

ONE OF THE EASIEST curtains to make is also one of the most versatile. Flat panel curtains are just pieces of fabric that are hemmed on all four edges and hung from decorative rods with clip-on or sew-on rings. That's as basic as you can get, yet this style of curtain can easily be adapted to create a variety of looks: unlined sheers or semisheers that cover the window, lined or unlined side panels that reveal most or all of the glass, panels formally styled into uniform folds, or panels allowed to casually drape and slouch.

Side framing (opposite)
Slouchy, casual curtain panels that puddle onto the floor are attached to wall hooks that echo the arch of the window frame. These curtains, drawn to the side with simple tiebacks, are stationary—the pleated shades provide the privacy and sun control.

Slim and trim (top)
Single widths of fabric, hemmed on all sides and hanging from crane rods, break up a window-wall covered with pleated shades. Such a simple treatment makes a big difference in the overall appearance of the room.

Simplicity (left)
Some windows need just a touch of fabric. These casual side panels, with their clean lines and neutral tone, conceal the window frame and enhance the padded cornice and pleated shade. So simple but so effective.

What you need to know

Flat panel curtains can be **designed** as simple, casual, sill-length panels; semi-formal floor-length styles, perfect for a contemporary interior; or spilling-onto-the-floor luxurious draperies. The look is strongly influenced by the *fullness* of the curtains, which can be sleek and spartan at one-and-one-half times fullness, full and opulent at three times fullness, or anywhere in between. See the examples for fullness and ring spacing on page 13.

Select firmly woven medium-weight **fabric** to create a simple tailored look, with an upper edge that can be styled into gentle rolling folds. Lightweight, slinky fabric will result in a relaxed, soft look, with an upper edge that dips gracefully between attachment points. Depending on the desired fullness, one full width of decorator fabric will cover an area 18" to 32" (46 to 81.5 cm) wide. If more width is desired, seam together full or half widths of fabric for each panel. You may prefer to line the curtain panels to add body and prevent the decorator fabric from fading.

The panels can be hung from a decorative rod with clip-on or sew-on curtain rings, which are available in many styles. Choose the hardware and **mount** the rod before you begin so you can accurately measure for the finished length. The rod is usually mounted above the window frame far enough that the top of the curtain covers the wood. Before you drill any holes, it is a good idea to *mock up* a small sample to determine the exact location of the curtain top in relation to the rod; the type of ring used also affects the measurement.

Materials

- Decorative curtain rod
- Tools and hardware for installation
- Decorator fabric
- Drapery lining for lined curtains
- Drapery weights for floor-length curtains
- Clip-on or sew-on rings

 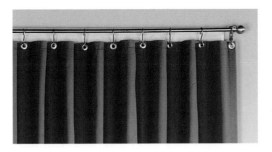 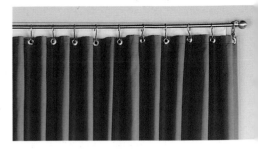

Different fabric fullnesses and same spacing between hooks For a flatter panel, one-and-one-half times fullness is used (left); this means the width of the curtain measures one-and-one-half times the length of the rod. For a fuller panel, use two times fullness (center) or two-and-one-half times fullness (right). In these photos, all rings are spaced 15½" (39.3 cm) apart.

Cutting directions

- The *cut length* of the fabric is equal to the finished length of the curtain plus the lower hem allowance (see chart below) plus 3" (7.5 cm) for the upper hem.

- The *cut width* of the fabric is equal to the amount of space you want to cover multiplied by the desired fullness (see examples above). Divide this amount by the width of the fabric and round up or down to the nearest whole or half width to find the number of fabric widths you need. Use full or half widths of fabric for each curtain panel.

- Multiply the cut length by the total number of widths needed to determine the amount of fabric to buy. Buy an extra *pattern repeat* per fabric width for matching patterns (page 123).

- For lined curtains, cut the lining fabric 5" (12.7 cm) shorter than the decorator fabric for floor-length curtains; 3" (7.5 cm) shorter than the decorator fabric for sill- or apron-length curtains; or the same length as the decorator fabric for curtains that puddle on the floor. The cut width of the lining is the same as the decorator fabric.

HEM ALLOWANCES	
Curtain length	Bottom hem allowance
to sill or apron	6" (15 cm)
½" (1.3 cm) above floor	8" (20.5 cm)
brushing floor	8" (20.5 cm)
puddling on floor	1" (2.5 cm)

Different spacing between rings and same fabric fullness For a controlled look along the top of the curtain, use more rings and space them close together (left). For a softer look, use fewer rings with more space between them (center). For dramatic swoops in the fabric, use a minimum of rings, spaced even farther apart (right). All of these curtain panels have two times fullness.

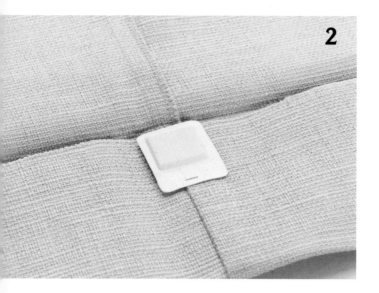

Making unlined flat panel curtains

1 Seam the fabric widths together, if necessary, for each curtain panel. If half widths are needed, add them at the sides of the panels. Finish the seams together, and press them toward the side of the panel.

2 Press under the lower edge the full amount of the hem allowance. Then unfold the pressed edge and turn the cut edge back, aligning it to the pressed fold line. Press the outer fold. If you are making floor-length curtains with more than one fabric width, tack a drapery weight to the upper layer of fabric at the base of each seam, with the bottom of the weight near the inner fold.

3 Refold the lower edge, forming a double-fold hem. Pin. Stitch, using a blindstitch for an invisible hem or a straight stitch for a visible hem.

4 Press under 3" (7.5 cm) on one side. Then unfold the pressed edge and turn the cut edge back, aligning it to the pressed fold line. Press the outer fold. If you are making floor-length curtains, insert a drapery weight between the layers of the lower hem and tack it in place. Refold the edge, forming a 1½" (3.8 cm) double-fold side hem. Stitch, using a blindstitch. Repeat for each side of each curtain panel.

5 Press under a 1½" (3.8 cm) double-fold hem in the upper edge. Stitch the upper hem.

6 Mark the placement for sew-on or clip-on rings along the top hem, placing the end marks ¾" (2 cm) from the sides. Space the remaining marks evenly 6" to 10" (15 to 25.5 cm) apart. Try different spacing patterns, using safety pins, to help you decide. See the examples on page 13. Attach a ring at each mark.

7 Slide the rings onto the drapery rod, and mount the rod on the brackets.

Making lined flat panel curtains

1 Follow steps 1 to 3 for unlined flat panel curtains on page 14. Repeat for the lining, but make a 2" (5 cm) double-fold hem in the lining.

2 Place the curtain panel and lining panel wrong sides together, matching the raw edges at the sides and upper edge; pin. The lining panel will be 1" (2.5 cm) shorter than the curtain panel. Complete the curtain as on page 14, steps 4 to 7, handling the decorator fabric and lining as one fabric.

Making puddled curtains

1 Follow step 1 on page 14 for both decorator fabric and lining. Place the lining and decorator fabric wrong sides together, matching the raw edges. Complete steps 2 to 7, treating both fabrics as one.

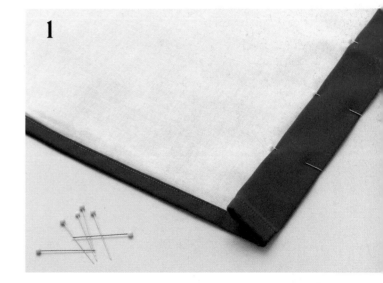

Grommet Curtains

FLAT CURTAIN PANELS with grommets in the top hem can be hung from a decorative rod with cording laced through the grommets or with fancy S-hooks. A popular look is curtains with very large grommets that are speared by the rod. A convenient grommet heading tape product, available in fabric stores, makes this project easy.

Muted geometrics (opposite)
Retro geometric patterns are back. The tones here are muted, so the pattern is not overwhelming. The grommet heading is threaded onto steel cables—totally chic.

Double up (top)
Sheers to filter sunlight and calm the breeze, sun-blocking panels for sleeping in late—these grommet curtains have it all. The casual puddling on the floor adds to the carefree attitude.

Accent on hardware (right)
Grommet tape, which comes with a choice of ring colors, assures uniform folds in these understated curtains. A boldly striped fabric is paired with a metal rod and sculpted finials; this treatment is as much about the hardware as it is the fabric.

What you need to know

Grommet curtains can be made in two styles: those with small grommets that are attached to the rod with hooks or cording, and those with large grommets that are speared by the rod. For either **design**, it is important to have an even number of grommets so both sides of the curtain can turn toward the wall. The space between grommets can be varied for small-grommet curtains. Closer spacing will hold the upper edge in a straighter line; wider spacing will allow the curtain to slouch between grommets. For large-grommet curtains, the space is determined by the grommet tape and cannot be altered. The tape has plastic spacer tabs that make the curtain top fold back and forth in gentle rolls and keep the upper edge straight.

Small-grommet curtains can be made from lightweight to medium-weight **fabric**. Lightweight slinky fabrics will slouch gracefully between grommets. Firmer fabric will hold a straighter line at the upper edge. To be sure the fabric is not too heavy, buy a small amount of fabric to test first; fold it into three layers, and attach a grommet. Use medium-weight fabric for grommet-tape curtains.

Before you cut into the fabric, **mount** the rod so you can take accurate measurements. To determine the proper height for the rod, *mock up* a sample the way you intend to hang the curtain, so you'll know the distance between the curtain top and the bottom of the rod for small-grommet curtains. For large-grommet curtains, the top of the rod will be even with the top of the grommet hole; the top of the curtain will be 1" (2.5 cm) above the rod.

Materials

- Decorative rod
- Tools and hardware for installation
- S-hooks for hanging curtain with small grommets
- Decorator fabric
- Drapery weights for floor-length curtains
- Drapery lining for lined curtains
- Safety pins
- Grommets, size 0 or $^1/_4$" (6 mm) and attaching tool for curtains with small grommets
- Grommet heading tape for curtains with large grommets

Cutting directions

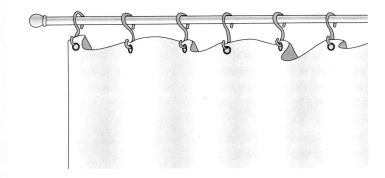

Small-grommet curtains

- The *cut length* of the fabric is equal to the finished length of the curtain plus the lower hem allowance (see chart on page 13) plus an upper hem allowance of two times the diameter of the grommet plus 2" (5 cm).

- The *cut width* of the fabric is equal to the amount of space you want to cover multiplied by the desired *fullness* (see examples on page 13). Divide this amount by the width of the fabric and round up or down to the nearest whole or half width, to determine the number of fabric widths you need. Use full or half widths of fabric for each curtain panel.

- Multiply the cut length by the total number of widths needed to determine the amount of fabric to buy. Buy an extra *pattern repeat* per fabric width for matching patterns.

Large-grommet curtains

- The *cut length* of the fabric is equal to the *finished length* of the curtain plus the lower hem allowance (see chart on page 13) plus 2" (5 cm) for the upper hem.

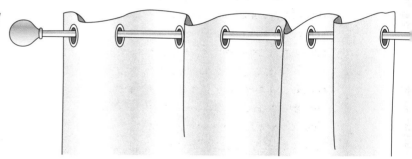

- The *finished width* of the curtain panel is equal to the amount of space you want to cover multiplied by two times fullness (required by the grommet tape). Measure this length of grommet tape. You must have an even number of grommets, and you must begin and end 2" (5 cm) beyond a space tab on each outer edge. Cut the grommet tape to this length.

- The *cut width* of the curtain panel is equal to the length of the grommet tape plus 6" (15 cm) for side hems. Divide this amount by the width of the fabric to determine the number of fabric widths you need. Don't cut the panel to the exact width until step 1 on page 20.

- Multiply the cut length by the total number of widths needed to determine the amount of fabric to buy. Buy an extra pattern repeat per fabric width for matching patterns.

Making curtains with small grommets

1 Follow steps 1 to 4 on page 14 for flat panel curtains. Press the double-fold hem into the upper edge. Unfold the fabric at the upper corners. Trim out the excess fabric of the side hem to within ⅜" (1 cm) of the first fold. Refold and stitch the upper hem.

2 Mark the placement for an even number of grommets along the top hem, placing the end marks ¾" (2 cm) from the sides. Space the remaining marks evenly 6" to 10" (15 to 25.5 cm) apart. Try different spacing patterns, using safety pins to help you decide.

3 Insert the grommets, following the manufacturer's directions.

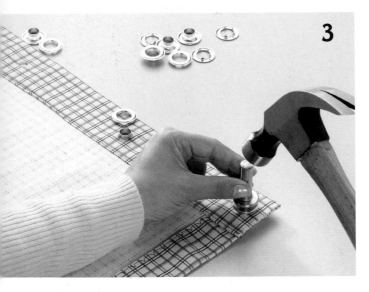

Making curtains with large grommets

1 Seam the fabric widths together, if necessary, for each curtain panel. Finish the seams together, and press them toward the side of the panel. Lay out the grommet tape along the upper edge of the panel, and adjust the placement so seams in the panel only fall between pairs of grommets that are spaced closer together. Mark the curtain panel 3" (7.5 cm) beyond the ends of the tape, and trim off excess fabric evenly down the sides.

2 Press under the lower edge the full amount of the hem allowance. Then unfold the pressed edge and turn the cut edge back, aligning it to the pressed fold line. Press the outer fold. If you are making floor-length curtains with more than one fabric width, tack a drapery weight to the upper layer of fabric at the base of each seam, with the bottom of the weight near the inner fold.

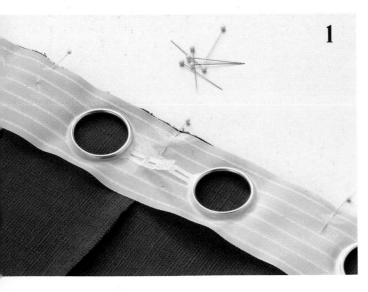

3 Refold the lower edge, forming a double-fold hem. Pin. Stitch, using a blindstitch for an invisible hem or a straight stitch for a visible hem.

4 Press under 3" (7.5 cm) on one side. Then unfold the pressed edge and turn the cut edge back, aligning it to the pressed fold line. Press the outer fold of the double-fold hem. Repeat on the other side. Unfold the side hems.

5 Turn under the upper edge 2" (5 cm) and press. Pin the grommet tape, tabs up, on the wrong side of the panel, aligning the cut ends to the inner folds of the side hems, with the upper edge of the tape 1½" (3.8 cm) from the upper pressed fold. Stitch close to the top and bottom edges of the tape.

6 Refold the side hems. Insert a drapery weight between the layers of the lower hem, and tack it in place. Stitch, using a blindstitch or straight stitch. Straight stitch the hems in place over the grommet tape, keeping the spacer tabs free.

7 Trim away the fabric from inside the grommet openings.

8 Working on a flat surface, clip the decorative rings over the grommet openings, encasing the raw edges of the fabric.

9 Hook the plastic spacers together to ripple-fold the curtain. Insert the rod through the grommets and hang the rod.

Curtains with Cuffs

AN ATTACHED CUFF of matching or contrasting fabric drapes gracefully along the top of a relaxed curtain. By varying the fullness or the way the curtains are hung, you can adapt this basic style to create different looks. Simply attach sew-on or clip-on rings to the upper edge and hang the curtain from a decorative rod or a series of interesting knobs or wall hooks. For a techno look, install grommets along the upper edge (page 20) and hang the curtain using cording or decorative hooks.

Dramatic draping (opposite)
The vibrant color and over-the-top styling of these curtains is in the same spirit as the art and furniture. Lavish draping makes the curtains sensuous and playful all at once. Hung from decorative wall hooks, the cuffs droop to reveal their contrast lining.

Feminine and pretty (top)
The tiny floral pattern of these semi-sheer curtains works so well with the wide stripes of the wallcovering and the floral-motif finials of the narrow rod. The curtains swish into shallow puddles on the floor. Their ruffly cuffed tops are edged with ribbon for a delicate finish.

Fringe benefits (left)
Bullion fringe caught in the seam traces the undulating curves of the burgundy silk cuffs that top off these citrine silk curtains. This lush treatment has a gilded ornate rod mounted close to the ceiling.

What you need to know

Cuffed curtains are a very casual and dramatic **design**. Because the upper edge slouches between hooks, the lower edge will also be uneven and should be allowed to break at or puddle on the floor. Use two or two-and-one-half times *fullness* and space the rings 12" to 16" (30.5 to 40.5 cm) apart for a gentle draping effect along the upper edge of the cuff. If you prefer a more controlled upper edge, use less fullness or space the grommets or rings closer together. The cuff length can range from 6" to 15" (15 to 38 cm) to suit the curtain length and the tone you want to create—short, casual, and perky to long, formal, and sophisticated.

Lightweight, drapable **fabrics** are most effective for this treatment, for both the curtain and cuff. If you want the curtain to hold a more rigid pattern of swoops and rolls, choose a firmer fabric so you will be able to arrange the cuffs a certain way. Lining the curtain and *interlining* the cuff with a lightweight drapery lining will also create more body.

Before you cut into the fabric, **mount** the rod or wall hooks so you can take accurate measurements. To determine the proper height for the hardware, *mock up* a sample the way you intend to hang the curtain, so you'll know the distance between the curtain top and the bottom of the rod or the hooks. For curtains that puddle on the floor, the exact length measurement is not as crucial.

Materials

- Decorative curtain rod
- Tools and hardware for installation
- Lightweight fabric that drapes softly for the curtain
- Matching or contrasting lightweight fabric for the cuff
- Drapery lining for lined curtains
- Drapery weights for floor-length curtains
- Clip-on or sew-on rings or grommets and attaching tool

Cutting directions

- The *cut length* of the fabric is equal to the finished length of the curtain plus the lower hem allowance (see chart on page 13) minus 2½" (6.5 cm). Include 2" (5 cm) for curtains that break at the floor or 12" to 20" (30.5 to 51 cm) for curtains that puddle on the floor.

- The *cut width* of the fabric is equal to the amount of space you want to cover multiplied by the desired fullness (see examples on page 13). Divide this amount by the width of the fabric and round up or down to the nearest whole or half width, to determine the number of fabric widths you need. Use full or half widths of fabric for each curtain panel.

- Multiply the cut length by the total number of widths needed to determine the amount of fabric to buy. Buy an extra *pattern repeat* per fabric width for matching patterns.

- The cut length of the cuff is equal to the finished length from the top of the curtain plus 3½" (9 cm) multiplied by 2. Use the same number of fabric widths as for the curtain, and seam them together so the cut width of the cuff is equal to the hemmed width of the curtain plus 1" (2.5 cm) for seam allowances on the sides.

- For lined curtains, cut the lining fabric 5" (12.7 cm) shorter than the decorator fabric for floor-length curtains; 3" (7.5 cm) shorter than the decorator fabric for sill- or apron-length curtains; or the same length as the decorator fabric for curtains that puddle on the floor. The cut width of the lining is the same as the decorator fabric.

Making curtains with cuffs

1 Seam the fabric widths together, if necessary, for each curtain panel. If half widths are needed, add them at the sides of the panels. Finish the seam allowances together, and press them toward the side of the panel.

2 Press under the lower edge the full amount of the hem allowance. Then unfold the pressed edge and turn the cut edge back, aligning it to the pressed fold line. Press the outer fold. If you are making floor-length curtains with more than one fabric width, tack a drapery weight to the upper layer of fabric at the base of each seam, with the bottom of the weight near the inner fold.

3 Refold the lower edge, forming a double-fold hem. Pin. Stitch, using a blindstitch for an invisible hem or a straight stitch for a visible hem. Omit steps 4 and 5 if the curtains are unlined.

4 For lined curtains, repeat steps 1 to 3 for the lining, making a 2" (5 cm) double-fold hem. For puddle curtains, layer the fabric and lining and treat them as one for hemming.

5 Place the curtain panel and lining panel wrong sides together, matching the raw edges at the sides and upper edge; pin. At the bottom, the lining panel will be 1" (2.5 cm) shorter than the curtain panel.

6 Press under 3" (7.5 cm) on one side. Then unfold the pressed edge and turn the cut edge back, aligning it to the pressed fold line. Press the outer fold. Insert a drapery weight between the layers of the lower hem, and tack it in place. Refold the edge, forming a 1½" (3.8 cm) double-fold side hem. Stitch, using a blindstitch. Repeat for each side of each curtain panel. If making lined curtains, treat the lining and face fabric as one.

7 Seam the fabric widths together for the cuff, using ½" (1.3 cm) seam allowances. Press the seams open. Fold the cuff in half crosswise, right sides together. Stitch ½" (1.3 cm) seams at the ends.

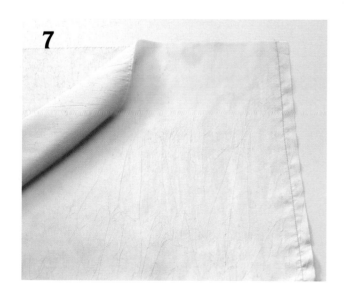

7

8 Turn the cuff right side out and press the seams at the ends. Baste the raw edges together and press along the fold.

9 Pin the cuff to the top of the curtain panel, matching raw edges, with the right side of the cuff facing down on the wrong side of the curtain panel. Stitch ½" (1.3 cm) seam; finish the seam, using zigzag or overlock stitch.

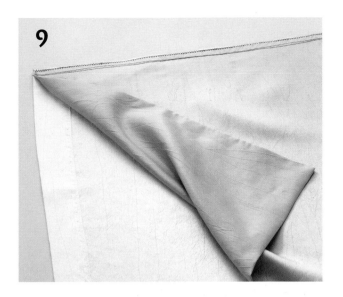

10 Fold the cuff 3" (7.5 cm) above the seam line as shown. Pin in place; do not press the fold.

11 Mark the upper fold ½" (1.3 cm) from each side of the curtain panel for the placement of the end grommets or rings.

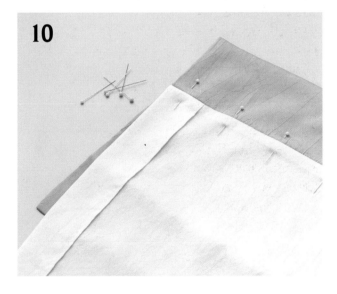

12 Mark the placement for the remaining grommets or rings 12" to 16" (30.5 to 40.5 cm) apart, spacing the marks evenly.

13 Install the grommets through all layers, with the top of each grommet ½" (1.3 cm) below the upper folded edge. Or secure clip-on rings or sew-on rings at markings. Remove the pins.

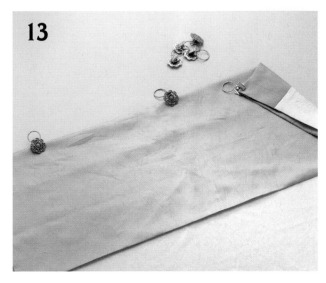

Tab Curtains

T HE EYE is drawn upward when a window is dressed with tab curtains. Narrow straps that loop or tie over a decorative rod give this treatment the no-frill appeal of blending form with function. The tabs can loop, tie, or be buttoned.

Classic country (opposite)
These sunny curtains for a country kitchen are floor-to-ceiling. Tied up simply with scarves that match the shade, these tab curtains are classic, uncluttered, and cheerful.

Retro with a twist (top)
The paisley panels of the seventies never looked this sophisticated. In updated styling, this decorator print is edged with a subtle geometric that is repeated in the slender tie tabs.

Tailored serenity (left)
Earth tones of cream, brown, and yellow create a calm and inviting space. Button accents on the tabs add just the right amount of detail to these understated curtains.

What you need to know

Tab curtains are not intended to be opened and closed repeatedly, because the friction would put too much strain on the tabs. Therefore, this curtain style is often **designed** as two stationary panels at the sides of a window. For a narrow window, one panel can cover the entire width at the top and be drawn to one side to let light in. The tabs can be a continuous loop, two straps that are tied over the rod, or a single strap attached at one end and seemingly buttoned to the curtain at the front. (To avoid strain on the buttons, the tabs are sewn in place and the buttons are just decorative.) Each fabric width has five or six evenly spaced tabs.

Tab curtains can be lined or unlined, depending on the **fabric** selection and the degree of light control and privacy required. Medium-weight decorator fabrics offer the needed strength for the tabs and will keep the upper edge of the curtain in a controlled line. If a soft drape between tabs is desired, choose a lighter weight, drapable fabric for the curtain.

It is wise to *mock up* the treatment and hang the rod before cutting for accurate length measurements (see the steps below). **Mount** the rod high enough so the top of the window frame will not be visible above the curtain.

Materials

- Decorative curtain rod
- Tools and hardware for installation
- Decorator fabric
- Drapery lining for lined curtains
- Drapery weights for floor-length curtains
- Buttons or covered button kits for button tab curtains

Measuring

1 Determine the tab length by wrapping a cloth tape measure over the rod the desired distance to the top of the curtain. Add 1" (2.5 cm) for seam allowances and 2¾" (7 cm) more for button tabs. For tie tabs, mock up a tab with wide ribbon or strips of fabric in the style of knot you want to use. Then measure the length of each piece and add 1" (2.5 cm) for end seams.

1

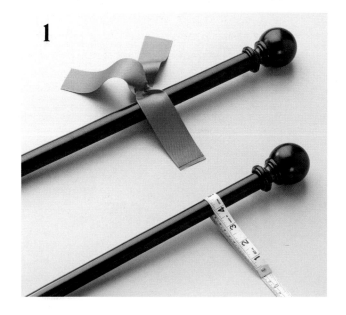

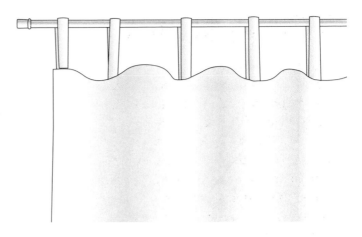

2 Measure the distance from the underside of the rod to the top of the curtain. Mount the rod a distance above the window equal to this distance plus 1" (2.5 cm). This ensures that the window frame will not show above the curtain.

Cutting directions

- The *cut length* of each curtain panel is equal to the finished length plus the bottom hem allowance (see chart on page 13) plus 3" (7.5 cm).

- The *cut width* of the fabric is equal to the amount of space you want to cover multiplied by 2. Divide this amount by the width of the fabric and round up or down to the nearest whole or half width, to determine the number of fabric widths you need. Use full or half widths of fabric for each curtain panel.

- For lined tab curtains, the cut length of the lining is equal to the finished length of the curtain plus 3½" (9 cm). The cut width is the same as for the decorator fabric.

- You will need five tabs for the first full width plus four tabs for each additional full width and two tabs for each additional half width in each curtain panel. For loop or button tabs 1½" (3.8 cm) wide, cut a 4" (10 cm) strip of fabric for each tab, using the length measurement from step 1, opposite. For tie tabs 1" (2.5 cm) wide, cut two 2½" (6.5 cm) strips for each tab, using the length measurement found in step 1, opposite.

- Multiply the cut length by the number of fabric widths needed to determine the total amount required for the curtains. For the tabs, add 12" (30.5 cm) for every two fabric widths needed to determine the total length to buy.

Making unlined loop tab curtains

1 Seam the fabric widths together as necessary for each curtain panel, adding any half widths at the *return* ends of the panels. Finish the seam allowances together, and press them toward the side of the panel.

2 Press under the lower edge 8" (20.5 cm) for the hem. Then unfold the pressed edge and turn the cut edge back, aligning it to the pressed fold line. Press the outer fold. If the panel has more than one fabric width, tack a drapery weight to the upper layer of fabric at the base of each seam, with the bottom of the weight near the inner fold.

3 Refold the lower edge, forming a 4" (10 cm) double-fold hem, encasing the weights at the seams. Pin. Stitch, using a blindstitch for an invisible hem or a straight stitch for a visible hem.

4 Press under ½" (1.3 cm) on the upper edge. Then fold 2" (5 cm) to the right side, forming a facing. At the outer corners, stitch the facing to the curtain 3" (7.5 cm) from the edges (arrow). Trim the facing to within ¼" (6 mm) of the stitching; trim off the top 1" (2.5 cm) of the side hem allowance (see photo on next page).

5 Fold each tab in half lengthwise, right sides together. Stitch a ½" (1.3 cm) seam along the cut edge.

(continued)

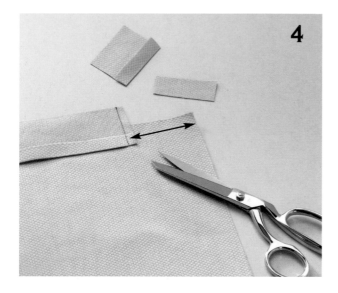

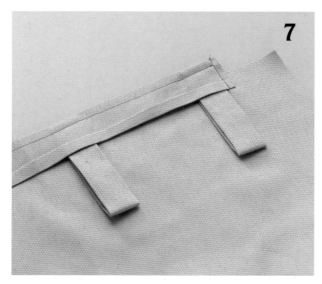

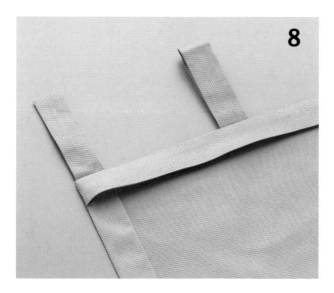

6 Turn the tabs right side out. Center the seam in the back of each tab; press.

7 Mark the placement for the tabs evenly spaced along the upper hem of the curtain, with the first and last tabs flush with the outer edges. Fold the tabs in half and slide them under the facing with the raw edges in the fold; pin. Stitch across the curtain top, ½" (1.3 cm) from the fold.

8 Press under 1½" (3.8 cm) double-fold side hems. Turn the facing to the curtain back; press. Stitch the side hems, encasing a drapery weight in the hem layers at the lower corners of floor-length curtains. At the upper corners, the hem will disappear under the facing. Stitch along the lower fold of the facing.

9 Hang the curtain from the rod. Space the tabs evenly on the rod. Train the curtain to fall in soft folds, with the fabric at the tabs rolling forward and the fabric between the tabs rolling toward the window.

Making lined tab curtains

1 Follow steps 1 to 3 for unlined tab curtains on page 31. Repeat for the lining, but make a 2" (5 cm) double-fold hem in the lining and omit drapery weights in the lining.

2 Place the curtain panel and lining panel wrong sides together, matching the raw edges at the sides. The upper edge of the lining will be 2½" (6.5 cm) below the upper edge of the curtain panel. At the bottom, the lining panel will be 1" (2.5 cm) shorter than the curtain panel. Pin.

3 Complete the curtain as on pages 31 and above, steps 4 to 9, handling the decorator fabric and lining as one fabric.

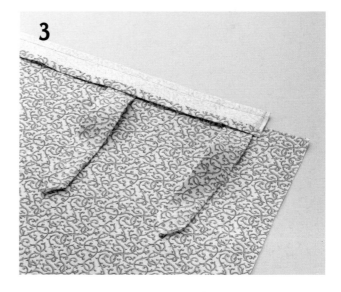

Making button tab curtains

1 Follow steps 1 to 5 on page 31. Center the seam in the back of the tab; press, avoiding sharp creases on the outer edges. Mark a point ¼" (6 mm) from the lower edge on the seam; mark points 1¼" (3.2 cm) from the lower edge on the outer folds.

2 Sew from the mark on the outer fold to the mark on the seam; pivot, and stitch to the mark on the opposite fold, forming the point of the tab. Trim the seam to ¼" (6 mm). Turn the tab right side out; press.

3 Follow step 7, but secure only the open end of the tabs under the facing, with the seam against the right side of the curtain.

4 Finish the curtains as in step 8. Turn the tabs down over the top of the curtain. Tack the tabs securely with the sewing machine. Sew buttons over the stitches. Hang the curtains as in step 9.

Making tie tab curtains

1 Follow steps 1 to 4 for loop tab curtains. Fold each tab in half lengthwise, right sides together. Stitch a ¼" (6 mm) seam along the cut edge and one end. Turn the tabs right side out and press.

2 Follow step 7, but stack two tabs, securing only the open ends under the facing.

3 Finish the curtains as in step 8. Hang the curtains as in step 9, tying the tabs over the rod.

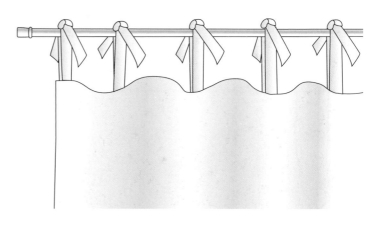

Scalloped Curtains

SCALLOPS EXAGGERATE the droops between tabs or rings along the upper edge of a curtain. The dips can be deep and dramatic on formal curtains that brush the floor or shallow and sweet on a set of café curtains. This style works for stationary curtains that are attached to a rod by tabs or by clip-on or sew-on rings. Curtains attached by rings can also traverse the rod to cover the window when necessary.

Black pinstripes (opposite)
Tall and tailored, scalloped curtains dress up and frame in the formal seating area of this greatroom. Pinstripes draw your eye upward to the scalloped, tabbed tops while seemingly raising the ceiling.

Café style (top)
Café curtains with scallop shaping and ribbon tie tabs are perfect in a room where light is necessary but privacy is, too. The blue and white print fabric is lined for added privacy, yet light can flood the room through the top window panes.

Filtered light (left)
Semisheer plaid curtains filter the morning sun streaming through bedroom windows. The curtains' scalloped upper edges droop softly between tie tabs, adding to the relaxed, laid-back atmosphere of the room.

What you need to know

For this **design**, you will need to make a paper pattern to shape the top of the curtain. For curtains with two panels that meet in the center, both panels should end with a tab or ring at the center edge. Seams are least visible if they are 3" (7.5 cm) from the nearest tab or ring. This will cause the scallop widths in the center of a multi-width panel to be slightly narrower than the other scallops. Scallop depths are all equal, however, and tabs or rings are spaced evenly along the rod, so the difference in scallop widths is not noticeable. Scalloped curtains can be lined or unlined, in a casual length just below the window frame, to a more formal length just above the floor, or breaking at the floor with 2" (5 cm) of extra length.

Select medium-weight **fabric** with enough body to hold the shape of the scallop. The scalloped edge is finished with a facing, using the same fabric as the curtain or a coordinating fabric.

Before **mounting** the rod above the window, consider the distance any rings or clips hang below the rod, as this will determine the highest point of the curtain's upper edge. If making tab curtains, wrap a cloth tape measure over the rod to determine the desired length of the tab. Also determine the depth of the scallops. Shallow scallops of 2½" to 3" (6.5 to 7.5 cm) work well for café curtains on a small window. Deep 8" (20.5 cm) scallops create a dramatic effect for floor-length curtains. Depending on how high the rod is mounted and the depth of the scallops, part of the upper window frame and even the glass may be exposed by the scallops.

Materials

- Decorative curtain rod
- Tools and hardware for installation
- Decorator fabric
- Matching or contrasting fabric for facing
- Matching or contrasting fabric for tabs, optional
- Paper, pencil, and string for making scallop pattern
- Drapery weights for floor-length curtains
- Drapery lining for lined curtains
- Clip-on or sew-on rings, optional
- Pin-on rings and cup hooks or tenter hooks for securing returns to wall

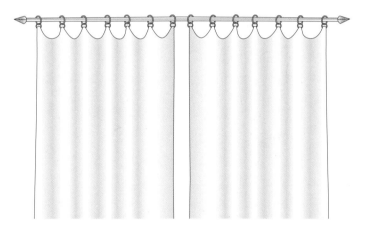

Cutting directions

- The *cut length* of the fabric is equal to the finished length of the curtain plus the bottom hem allowance (see chart on page 13) plus ½" (1.3 cm) for the seam allowance at the upper edge.

- The *cut width* of the fabric is equal to the amount of space you want to cover multiplied by two times *fullness*. Divide this amount by the width of

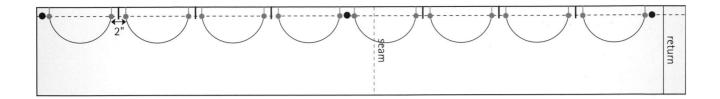

the fabric and round up or down to the nearest whole or half width, to find the number of fabric widths you need. Use full or half widths of fabric for each curtain panel.

- Cut fabric for the facing, with the length equal to the scallop depth plus 4" (10 cm) and the width equal to the cut width of the curtain fabric.

- The cut length of the lining is equal to the cut length of the decorator fabric minus the scallop depth minus 8" (20.5 cm).

- If making tab curtains, cut a 3" (7.5 cm) strip of fabric for each tab, 1" (2.5 cm) longer than the desired finished length. You will need five tabs for the first full width plus four tabs for each additional full width and two tabs for each additional half width in each curtain panel.

- Cut paper for the pattern, 2" (5 cm) longer than the desired scallop depth and 6" (15 cm) narrower than the seamed width of the curtain panel. This equals the finished width of the curtain after hemming.

Making unlined scalloped curtains

1 Seam the fabric widths together as necessary for each curtain panel, adding any half widths at the *return* ends of the panels. Repeat for the facings. Finish the seam allowances together, and press them toward the side of the panel.

2 Press under the lower edge 8" (20.5 cm) for the hem. Then unfold the pressed edge and turn the cut edge back, aligning it to the pressed fold line. Press the outer fold. For floor-length curtains, if the panel has more than one fabric width,

tack a drapery weight to the upper layer of fabric at the base of each seam, with the bottom of the weight near the inner fold.

3 Refold the lower edge, forming a 4" (10 cm) double-fold hem, encasing the weights at the seams. Pin. Stitch, using a blindstitch for an invisible hem or a straight stitch for a visible hem.

4 Finish the lower edge of the facing by serging, or turn the edge under ¼" (6 mm) twice and stitch.

5 Mark a ½" (1.3 cm) seam allowance across the upper edge of the pattern. Mark the depth of the return on one end of the pattern; mark the seam positions.

6 Mark a point on the upper seam line ½" (1.3 cm) away from the return. Mark a point 3" (7.5 cm) beyond the first seam from the return.

7 Fold the paper to divide the space between marks into four equal parts if the space represents a whole width, or into two equal parts if the space represents a half width; crease to mark. Unfold.

8 Divide any additional whole widths, falling between the return end and the opposite end of the panel, into four equal parts, placing the marks for the tabs or rings nearest the seams 3" (7.5 cm) beyond the seams.

9 Mark a point ½" (1.3 cm) from the end; divide the end width into four equal parts.

10 Mark the scallop end points on the upper seam line, 1" (2.5 cm) on each side of the marks. This allows for ½" (1.3 cm) seam allowances in the scalloped edge and 1" (2.5 cm) space for the tabs or rings.

(continued)

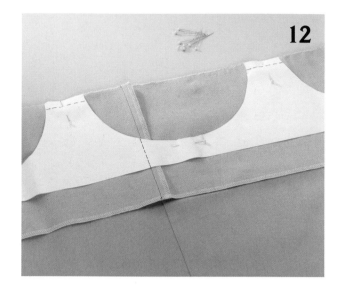

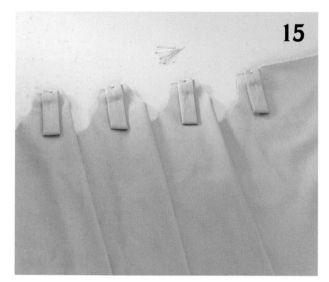

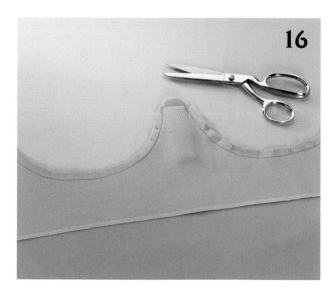

11 Mark the depth of the scallop in the first space from the return, measuring from the upper edge of the pattern; draw the scallop from the end points through the depth mark. Refold, and cut the first set of scallops. Repeat for each set of scallops.

12 Place the facing over the curtain panel, right sides together, matching the upper and side edges. Pin the pattern over the facing, aligning the upper edges and seam marks; cut the scallops through both layers. Transfer the mark for the return. Remove the facing. For curtains without tabs, omit steps 13 to 15.

13 Fold each tab in half lengthwise, right sides together. Stitch a ½" (1.3 cm) seam along the cut edge.

14 Turn the tabs right side out. Center the seam in the back of each tab; press.

15 Fold each tab in half, aligning the raw edges. Pin or baste the tabs in place on the right side of the curtain, aligning the raw edges of the tabs to the upper edge of the curtain and centering the tabs between the scallops. Pin the tab at the return end with the outer edges on the return mark. Pin the tab at the opposite end 3" (7.5 cm) from the side of the panel.

16 Pin the facing to the upper edge of the curtain, right sides together, aligning the raw edges. Stitch a ½" (1.3 cm) seam. A zipper foot may be used to stitch close to the tab. Trim the seam; clip the curves. Turn the curtain right side out, aligning the outer raw edges; press.

17 Press under 3" (7.5 cm) on one side. Then unfold the pressed edge and turn the cut edge back, aligning it to the pressed fold line. Press the outer fold. Insert a drapery weight between the layers of the lower hem, and tack it in place. Refold the edge, forming a 1½" (3.8 cm) double-fold side hem. Stitch, using a blindstitch. Repeat for each side of each curtain panel. Fold the hem under diagonally at the upper corners, if necessary; hand-stitch.

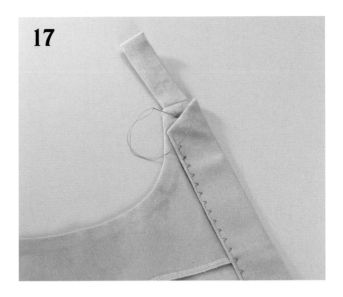

18 Hang the curtain from the rod, using tabs or clip-on or sew-on rings. Attach a pin-on ring to the inner edge of the return, and secure it to a tenter hook or cup hook in the wall.

19 Space the tabs or rings evenly on the rod. Train the curtain so the fabric in the scallops rolls toward the window; fabric at the tabs or rings rolls outward, forming soft folds.

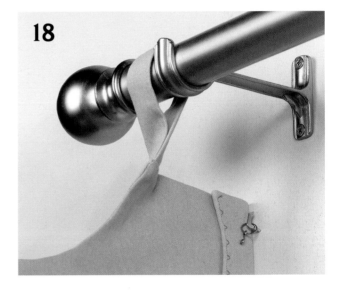

Making lined scalloped curtains

1 Follow steps 1 to 3 for unlined scalloped curtains on page 37. Repeat for the lining, but make a 2" (5 cm) double-fold hem in the lining and omit drapery weights in the lining.

2 Pin the facing to the upper edge of the lining, right sides together. Stitch a ½" (1.3 cm) seam. Press the seam allowances toward the facing.

3 Follow steps 5 to 16 on pages 37 and 38. Align the outer edges of the facing and lining to the outer edges of the curtain. The lining will be 1" (2.5 cm) shorter than the curtain panel. Complete the curtain, following steps 17 to 19, folding the lining and decorator fabric as one.

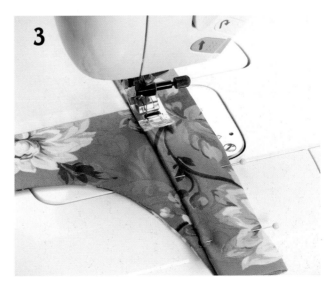

Styling Tape Curtains

CLEVER AND PRACTICAL, styling tapes help even rookie sewers create curtains with gorgeous, intricate headings. The tapes have woven-in cords that are pulled to draw the fabric fullness into pleats, gathers, or distinctive folds. Some tape styles imitate European hand-smocking; some create tiny, continuous pencil pleats; others fold the fabric into three-finger pinch pleats—all at a tug of the cords!

Well-dressed bay (opposite)
Window walls, like this expansive bay, can be a design challenge. Multiple layers at the window make the room cozy. Only the underlayer needs to open and close. The sumptuous curtains have a styling tape heading accented with a contrasting fabric band.

Delightful dining room (top)
The cheerful cabbage rose pattern of these tied-back curtains creates an inviting atmosphere for dining. The smocked curtain heading, mounted just under the crown molding, was created effortlessly with styling tape.

Exotic silk (left)
Semisheer silk curtains with a wide shirred heading are global-chic. Styling tape made the sewing quick and easy.

What you need to know

Styling tapes in various pleating and gathering styles are available in the decorating areas of fabric stores as precut packaged lengths or to be bought by the yard. Instructions for using the tape are included to help you **design** your curtains. The amount of *fullness* needed in the curtain depends on the style of tape you select—most require two to three times fullness.

For best results, use medium-weight to lightweight **fabric**.

Mount the hardware before you cut to ensure accurate measurements. The curtains can be installed on standard or decorative curtain rods or on pole sets with rings. Some tapes have loops woven into them for securing drapery pins, and some manufacturers provide special pins for installation.

Materials

- Standard curtain rod, decorative rod, or pole set with rings
- Tools and hardware for installation
- Decorator fabric
- Drapery weights
- Styling tape
- Thin cardboard
- 2 small plastic bags
- Drapery hooks

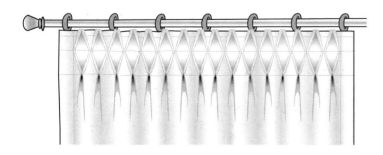

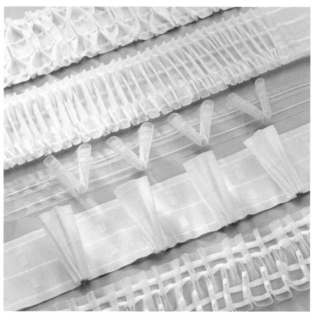

Styling tapes

Cutting directions

- The *cut length* of the decorator fabric is equal to the desired *finished length* of the curtain plus the bottom hem allowance (see chart on page 13) plus ¾" (2 cm) for turn-under at the upper edge. If using a standard curtain rod, measure the finished length of the curtain from the top of the rod; then add ½" (1.3 cm) so the curtain will extend above the rod. If using a decorative curtain rod or a pole set with rings, measure the length from the pin holes in the slides or rings.

- The *cut width* of the fabric is equal to the width to be covered multiplied by the recommended fullness of the styling tape plus 6" (15 cm) for side hems. If it is necessary to seam the fabric widths together to make each panel, allow 1" (2.5 cm) for each seam. If a standard or decorative curtain rod is used, also add twice the *projection* of the rod for *returns*.

- The cut length of the lining is 5¾" (14.5 cm) shorter than the cut length of the decorator fabric. The cut width of the lining is the same as the decorator fabric.

Making styling tape curtains

1 Seam fabric widths together, if necessary, for each panel. Finish the seam allowances together, and press them toward the side of the panel.

2 Press under the lower edge the full amount of the hem allowance. Then unfold the pressed edge and turn the cut edge back, aligning it to the pressed fold line. Press the outer fold. If you are making floor-length curtains with more than one fabric width, tack a drapery weight to the upper layer of fabric at the base of each seam, with the bottom of the weight near the inner fold.

3 Refold the lower edge, forming a double-fold hem, encasing the weights at the seams. Pin. Stitch, using a blindstitch for an invisible hem or a straight stitch for a visible hem.

4 Press under 3" (7.5 cm) on one side. Then unfold the pressed edge and turn the cut edge back, aligning it to the pressed fold line. Press the outer fold. Insert a drapery weight between the layers of the lower hem, and tack it in place. Refold the edge, forming a 1½" (3.8 cm) double-fold side hem. Repeat for each side of each curtain panel.

5 Press under ¾" (2 cm) on the upper edge of the curtain panel. Cut the styling tape to the width of the hemmed panel plus 2" (5 cm). Turn under 1" (2.5 cm) on each end of the tape, and use a pin to pick out the cords. Position the tape right side up on the wrong side of the panel, with the upper edge of the tape ¼" (6 mm) from the top.

6 Stitch the tape to the curtain, stitching just inside the top and bottom edges and next to any additional cords.

7 Knot all cords together, or knot them in pairs, at each end of the styling tape. At one end, pull evenly on the cords to pleat or gather the curtain panel to its determined finished width.

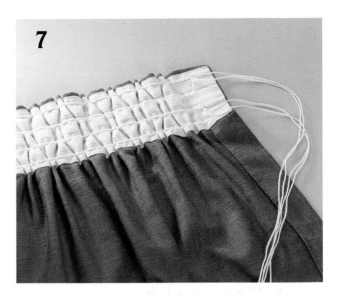

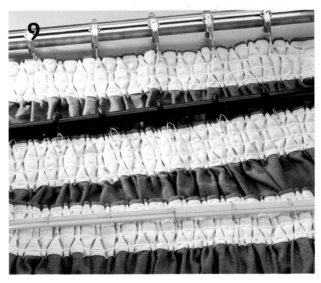

8 Knot the cords securely at the side. Wind the excess cord around a square of thin cardboard, and tuck it into a small plastic bag pinned to the side hem out of sight.

9 Insert drapery pins at the ends of the panels and at 3" (7.5 cm) intervals. If the styling tape has loops, insert drapery pins into them. Insert the drapery pins into the eyes of the slides on a decorative curtain rod (top) or the eyes of the rings for a pole set (middle). Or use drapery pins with round tops and hook them over a standard curtain rod.

43

Classic Rod-Pocket Curtains

ROD-POCKET curtains are often chosen for a stationary window treatment that is stylish and easy to sew. With ample fullness and a deep, ruffly heading, classic rod-pocket curtains take on a feminine, romantic appearance. With less fullness and a shorter heading, the look becomes more tailored and modern. Either way, the fluid lines and gathered fabric soften the hard surfaces and edges of the window.

Sunny sheers (opposite)
These sheer rod-pocket curtains bring sunshine into this quaint bedroom. The vibrant yellow is tempered by the blue (the complementary color) of the walls, Roman shade, and bedding. With their short heading and spilling-onto-the-floor length, this treatment is definitely a departure from the rod-pocket curtains of the past.

Classic florals (top)
Rod-pocket side panels mounted over traversing draperies create a soft focal point for this bedroom. Sewn from pretty floral fabric, they have a modest heading, and the inner edges are accented with decorator ball fringe.

Retro linens (right)
These curtains were made from colorful tablecloths in patterns from the forties. Cinched with fruit ties that conjure up Carmen Miranda, they make a bold statement in this charming kitchen.

What you need to know

Rod-pocket curtains have a *heading* and *rod pocket*. The heading is the portion at the top of a rod-pocket curtain that forms a ruffle when the curtain is on the rod. The depth of the heading is the distance from the top of the curtain to the top stitching line of the rod pocket. The rod pocket is the "tunnel" where the rod or pole is inserted; stitching lines at the top and bottom of the rod pocket keep the rod in place. To determine the depth of the rod pocket, measure around the widest part of the rod or pole; add ½" (1.3 cm) ease to this measurement, and divide by two.

To **design** your rod-pocket curtains, first decide how you will hang them. Several types of rods can be used, including flat rods in widths of 1", 2½", and 4½" (2.5, 6.5, and 11.5 cm). Wood and metal pole sets with elbows or finials can also be used and are available in several diameters. When a curtain rod or pole set with elbows is used, sides of the curtain panels wrap to the wall. This portion is called the *return*. For curtains mounted on poles with finials, returns can be created by making an opening in the front of the rod pocket for inserting the pole.

Rod-pocket curtains work well with a variety of **fabrics**. Unlined rod-pocket curtains can be made from sheers or laces, creating a lightweight treatment that allows filtered light to enter the room. For curtains made from medium-weight decorator fabrics, lining can be used to make the curtains more durable and opaque, add extra body, and support the side hems and heading. For sheer fabrics, allow two-and-one-half to three times the length of the rod for *fullness*; for heavier fabrics, allow two to two-and-one-half times.

Before cutting the fabric, decide where the window treatment should be positioned and **mount** the curtain rod or pole. Brackets are usually mounted on the wall just outside the window frame so the bottom of the rod is even with the top of the frame. Measure from the lower edge of the rod to where you want the lower edge of the curtain. To determine the *finished length* of the curtain, add the desired depth of the heading and rod pocket to this measurement.

Materials

- Standard curtain rod or pole set with finials or elbows
- Tools and hardware for installation
- Decorator fabric
- Drapery lining for lined curtains
- Drapery weights for floor-length curtains
- Fusible interfacing

Cutting directions

- The *cut length* of the fabric is equal to the finished length of the curtain plus the lower hem allowance (see chart on page 13) plus the depth of the heading and the rod pocket plus ½" (1.3 cm) for turn-under at the upper edge.

- The *cut width* of the fabric is equal to the amount of space you want to cover (including returns) multiplied by the desired fullness. Divide this amount by the width of the fabric and round up or down to the nearest whole or half width to find the number of fabric widths you need. Use full or half widths of fabric for each curtain panel.

- Multiply the cut length by the total number of widths needed to determine the amount of fabric to buy. Buy an extra *pattern repeat* per fabric width for matching patterns (page 123).

- For lined curtains, cut the lining fabric 5" (12.7 cm) shorter than the decorator fabric. The cut width of the lining is the same as the decorator fabric.

Making unlined rod-pocket curtains

1 Seam the fabric widths together, if necessary, for each curtain panel. If half widths are needed, add them at the sides of the panels. Finish the seam allowances together, and press them toward the side of the panel.

2 Press under the lower edge the full amount of the hem allowance. Then unfold the pressed edge and turn the cut edge back, aligning it to the pressed fold line. Press the outer fold. If you are making floor-length curtains with more than one fabric width, tack a drapery weight to the upper layer of fabric at the base of each seam, with the bottom of the weight near the inner fold.

(continued)

3 Refold the lower edge, forming a double-fold hem, encasing the weights at the seams. Pin. Stitch, using a blindstitch for an invisible hem or a straight stitch for a visible hem.

4 Press under 3" (7.5 cm) on one side. Then unfold the pressed edge and turn the cut edge back, aligning it to the pressed fold line. Press the outer fold. Insert a drapery weight between the layers of the lower hem, and tack it in place. Refold the edge, forming a 1½" (3.8 cm) double-fold side hem. Stitch, using a blindstitch. Repeat for each side of each curtain panel.

5 Press under ½" (1.3 cm) on the upper edge. Then press under an amount equal to the rod-pocket depth plus the heading depth. If the curtain will be mounted on a pole with elbow returns, omit steps 6 to 8.

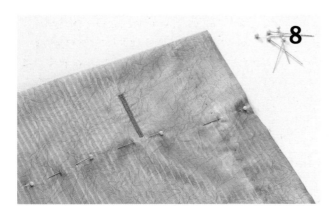

6 Mount the rod on a wooden, keyhole, or elbow bracket. Measure the distance from the wall to the center of the pole.

7 Unfold the upper edge of the curtain on the return side of the panel. On the right side of the fabric, measure from the side of the curtain a distance equal to the measurement in step 6; mark at the center of the rod pocket. If the curtain will be mounted on a rod with keyhole brackets, omit step 8.

8 Cut a 1" (2.5 cm) strip of fusible interfacing, 1" (2.5 cm) longer than the depth of the rod pocket. Fuse the strip to the wrong side of the curtain panel, centering it directly under the mark made in step 7. On the right side of the panel, stitch a buttonhole at the mark, from the top to the bottom of the rod pocket. Refold the upper edge of the panel along the pressed lines; pin.

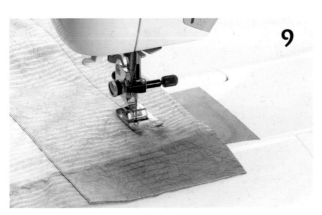

9 Stitch close to the first fold; stitch again at the depth of the heading, using tape on the bed of the sewing machine as a stitching guide.

Making lined rod-pocket curtains

1 Follow steps 1 to 3 for unlined rod-pocket curtains on page 47. Repeat for the lining, but make a 2" (5 cm) double-fold hem in the lining and omit drapery weights in the lining.

2 Place the curtain panel and lining panel wrong sides together, matching the raw edges at the sides and upper edge; pin. At the bottom, the lining panel will be 1" (2.5 cm) shorter than the curtain panel. Complete the curtain as on page 48, steps 4 to 9, handling the decorator fabric and lining as one fabric.

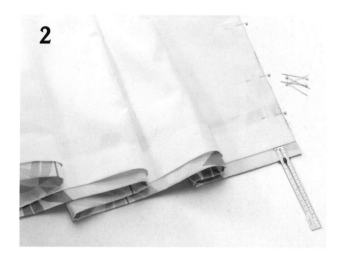

Installing rod-pocket curtains

Pole with wooden brackets and finials (left)
Remove the finials; insert the pole into the rod pocket with ends of the pole extending through the buttonholes. Reattach the finials; mount the pole. Secure the return to the wooden bracket, using self-adhesive hook and loop tape.

Pole with keyhole bracket and finials (center)
Slit the center of the rod pocket at the point marked in step 7, opposite. Insert the pole into the pocket.

Pull the return over the end of pole, aligning slit to the finial screw hole; attach the finials through the slits, and mount the pole. Attach a pin-on ring to the inner edge of the return and secure to a cup hook or tenter hook in wall.

Pole with elbows (right)
Insert the pole through the rod pocket; pull the curtain back to expose the small screws. Mount the pole on brackets. Slide the curtain over brackets.

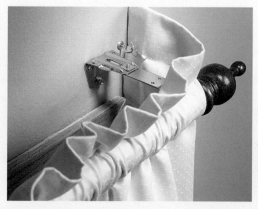

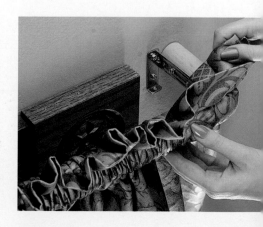

Rod-Pocket Curtains with Fancy Headings

EASY CHANGES in the headings of rod-pocket curtains can change their look. For some styles, such as a flounce heading or a popped heading, a softer, more feminine look is created by simply increasing the depth of the heading and shaping it on the rod. With a few extra steps, you can make a contrasting flounce or a welted heading, changing an ordinary rod-pocket curtain into an impressive room accent. Make the heading extra long and shape it to a point in the center, and you have a waterfall.

Intimate setting (opposite)
Lush rod-pocket curtains in a gold-tone fabric—always a popular color—make this small dining area feel intimate. The extending heading falls gently forward, topping off the low-slung side panels with casual grace. The effect is not overpowering—just a nice focal point.

Popped heading (top)
Decorators are incorporating fashion details into window treatments—like these popped headings that could be on an evening gown at the Oscars! The elegantly feminine treatment is perfect for this boudoir.

Waterfall headings (left)
The contrasting, extended headings on these rod-pocket curtains, often called waterfalls, are the crowning glory of this otherwise plain window treatment. As a strong design element, they tie together the two stories of windows, making the large space cozier.

What you need to know

Here are some guidelines to help you **design** this treatment:

• A popped *heading* is created by pulling the layers of the heading apart after inserting the rod into the pocket. Allow a heading depth of 6" to 8" (15 to 20.5 cm). Do not press the upper edge of the curtain when turning under the heading and rod-pocket depth.

• An extended heading drapes down over the front of the rod pocket, creating a short flounce, a mock valance, or a much longer waterfall. Allow a heading depth of 12" to 16" (30.5 to 40.5 cm) for a flounce or mock valance; up to 36" (91.5 cm) for a waterfall.

• A contrasting flounce, mock valance, or waterfall can repeat a fabric that is used in the tieback for a coordinated look. A separate facing of contrasting fabric is sewn to the curtain at the top of the heading.

• A welted heading, measuring 4" to 6" (10 to 15 cm) deep, droops into dramatic curves above the rod pocket. Contrasting welting is sewn into the seam at the top of the heading between the curtain and the facing.

Use medium-weight **fabrics** that have enough body to hold the shape of extended or popped headings. Lining adds body to flounce and welted headings and prevents show-through when a light-colored fabric is used. Sheer or semisheer fabric with body can be used for a curtain with a popped heading.

Refer to rod-pocket curtains (page 46) for how to measure the depth of the rod pocket and heading, where to **mount** the rod, and how to measure for finished length.

Cutting directions

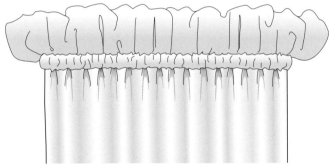

Popped heading

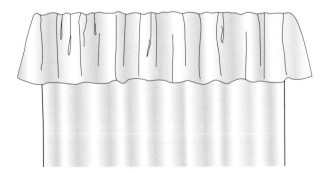

Flounce heading

Popped, flounce, mock valance, or waterfall heading

• Cut the decorator fabric and lining as for rod pocket curtains on page 47; allow for heading depths as given ar left.

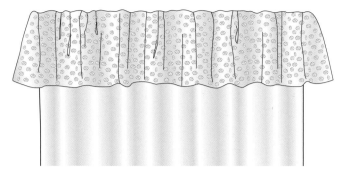

Contrasting flounce heading

Contrasting flounce, mock valance, or waterfall heading

- The *cut length* is equal to the desired finished length of the curtain plus the hem allowance plus the rod-pocket depth plus the extended heading allowance plus ½" (1.3 cm) for the seam allowance at the top.

- The *cut width* is the same as for other rod-pocket curtains (page 47).

- Cut the fabric for the heading facing with the length equal to the depth of the heading plus the depth of the rod pocket plus 1" (2.5 cm) for turn-under and seam allowance. The cut width of the facing is the same as the cut width of the decorator fabric.

- Cut the lining fabric 5" (12.7 cm) shorter than the decorator fabric. The cut width of the lining is the same as the decorator fabric.

Welted heading

- Cut the decorator fabric, facing, and lining as for rod-pocket curtains with a contrasting flounce, mock valance, or waterfall heading.

- From contrasting fabric, cut bias fabric strips, 1⅝" (4 cm) wide, to cover the cording for the welting.

- For lined curtains, cut the lining fabric 5" (12.7 cm) shorter than the decorator fabric for floor-length curtains; 3" (7.5 cm) shorter than the decorator fabric for sill- or apron-length curtains; the same length as the decorator fabric for curtains that puddle on the floor. The cut width of the lining is the same as the decorator fabric.

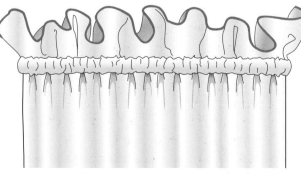

Welted heading

Making a contrasting extended heading

1 Follow steps 1 to 3 for unlined rod-pocket curtains on page 47. Repeat for the lining, but make a 2" (5 cm) double-fold hem in the lining and omit drapery weights in the lining.

2 Place the curtain panel and lining panel wrong sides together, matching the raw edges at the sides and upper edge; pin. At the bottom, the lining panel will be 1" (2.5 cm) shorter than the curtain panel.

3 Pin the facing to the top of the curtain panel, right sides together; if the facing fabric has a one-way design, make sure it will run in the right direction when the flounce falls forward. Stitch a ½" (1.3 cm) seam; press the seam open.

4 Press under 1½" (3.8 cm) twice on the sides, folding the lining and curtain fabric as one. Open out the hem, and trim the facing seam allowance in the hem area. Tack drapery weights inside the side hems, about 3" (7.5 cm) from the lower edge. Stitch to make double-fold side hems.

5 Press under ½" (1.3 cm) on the lower edge of the facing. Turn under the facing along the seam line; press. Pin the facing to the curtain panel along the pressed edge. Mark the upper stitching line for the rod pocket on the facing. Pin along the line to keep all the layers together.

6 Stitch close to the lower pressed edge. Stitch again along the marked line, creating the rod pocket.

7 Insert the rod or pole through the rod pocket. Mount the rod or pole on the brackets, draping the flounce toward the front, and arrange the gathers.

Making a welted heading

1 Seam the bias fabric strips together. Center the cording on the wrong side of the fabric strip, with the end of the cording 1" (2.5 cm) from the end of the strip; fold the end of the strip back over the cording.

2 Fold the fabric strip around the cording, wrong sides together, matching the raw edges and encasing the end of the cording.

3 Machine-baste close to the cording, using a zipper foot or welting foot, to create welting.

4 Follow steps 1 and 2 opposite. Stitch the welting to the right side of the curtain at the upper edge, matching raw edges; place the encased end of the welting 3" (7.5 cm) from the side of the panel. Stop stitching 5" (12.7 cm) from the opposite side of the panel.

5 Mark the upper edge of the curtain 3" (7.5 cm) from the side; cut the welting 1" (2.5 cm) beyond the mark.

6 Remove the stitching from the end of the welting, and cut the cording even with the mark on the curtain panel.

7 Fold the end of the fabric strip over the cording, encasing the end of the cording. Finish stitching the welting to the curtain panel, stopping 3" (7.5 cm) from the side.

8 Follow steps 3 and 4 on page 54 for the contrasting flounce. When stitching side hems, stitch up to the welting and secure the threads; start stitching again on the other side of the welting.

9 Complete the curtains as in steps 5 and 6, opposite. Insert the rod through the pocket, gathering the fabric evenly. Mount the rod.

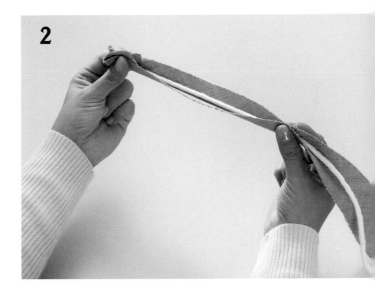

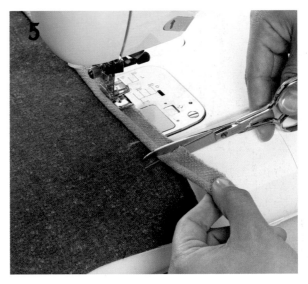

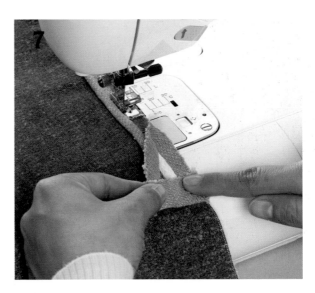

Ruffled Rod-Pocket Curtains

RUFFLES ARE FRILLY, feminine, and charming. The look can be relaxed and luxurious in floor-length silk curtains for a master suite or fresh and cute for a nursery or little girl's room.

Feminine floral (opposite)
Lined rod-pocket curtains with ruffles along the inner edges and bottom dress a simple casement window in a guest bedroom. A layer of eyelet trim added to the ruffle is a sweet touch. Tiebacks in the same plaid as the ruffle are a contrasting companion to the floral print.

Pristine white (top)
Floor-length, semisheer, ruffled curtains enhance the inviting outdoor view from this cozy cottage bedroom. Shades behind the curtains provide the light control and privacy when needed.

Country clever (right)
Simple ruffled curtains work well in a country-style kitchen. Small windows like these can't handle anything heavier or more imposing than this wispy, sheer treatment. So the windows can open in, the curtains are mounted directly onto the window frames.

What you need to know

The instructions that follow are for lined rod-pocket curtains with a self-faced ruffle along one edge and the bottom of each panel. You can **design** your curtains as one panel pulled back to the side with a tieback or holdback or as two panels that meet in the middle and are pulled back to the sides. The *return* sides are not ruffled. When two panels meet in the middle, the heights of the ruffles are staggered so one laps over the other from the *rod pocket* to the top of the *heading*. The width of the ruffle is a matter of personal taste and the look you want to achieve. Narrow ruffles simply accent the curtain edges, much like fringe. Longer ruffles make a more romantic statement.

Use lightweight to medium-weight **fabrics** for both the curtain and ruffle, using less *fullness* for heavier fabric to accommodate the bulk of the ruffle seam. Soft, drapable fabric will give the ruffles a luxurious droop. Crisp fabrics make perkier ruffles.

Follow the guidelines for classic rod-pocket curtains (page 46) for **mounting** the hardware and measuring the treatment.

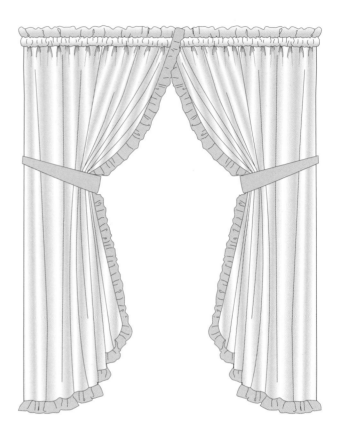

Materials

- Standard curtain rod or pole set with finials or elbows
- Tools and hardware for installation
- Decorator fabric for curtain
- Matching or contrasting fabric for ruffle
- Drapery lining
- Heavy thread or cord, such as crochet cord
- Pencil and string
- Drapery weights for floor-length curtains

Cutting directions

- The *cut length* of the curtain is equal to the *finished length* minus the finished width of the ruffle plus the depth of the rod pocket and heading plus 1" (2.5 cm) for seam allowance and turn-under.

- The *cut width* of the fabric is equal to the amount of space you want to cover multiplied by the desired fullness. Divide this amount by the width of the fabric and round up or down to the nearest whole or half width to determine the number of fabric widths you need. Use full or half widths of fabric for each curtain panel.

- Cut the lining for each panel to the same length and width as the decorator fabric.

- Cut fabric strips for the ruffles on the *lengthwise* or *crosswise grain* of the fabric with the width equal to twice the desired finished width plus 1" (2.5 cm). Cut as many strips as necessary for a continuous length of two to two-and-one-half times the length to be ruffled.

Making ruffled lined rod-pocket curtains

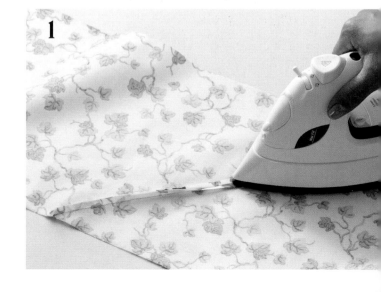

1 Pin two ruffle strips right sides together at right angles to each other, with the short ends extending ¼" (6 mm). Mark a diagonal line connecting the inner intersecting corners. Stitch. Trim the excess fabric to within ¼" (6 mm) of the stitching line. Press the seam allowances open. The diagonal seam minimizes the bulk.

2 Repeat step 1 to join all the ruffle strips. Fold the ends of the strip in half lengthwise, right sides together, and stitch across the ends in ¼" (6 mm) seams. Turn the ruffle strip right side out, aligning the raw edges, and press.

(continued)

3 Zigzag over a cord within the ½" (1.3 cm) seam allowance, stitching through both layers of the ruffle strip.

4 Seam the fabric widths together, if necessary, for each curtain panel. If half widths are needed, add them at the sides of the panels. Finish the seam allowances together, and press them toward the side of the panel.

5 Repeat step 4 for the lining panels.

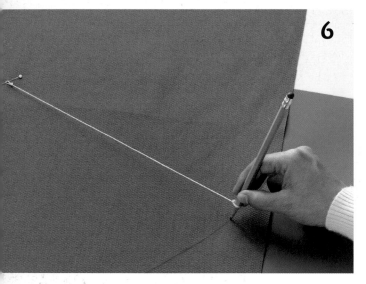

6 Mark a curve on the inside lower edge of one curtain panel with a pencil and string from a pivot point 12" (30.5 cm) up from the bottom and 12" (30.5 cm) in from the side.

7 Place the curtain panel over the lining, wrong sides together, matching the edges. Cut along the marked line through both layers. If your curtain has two panels, curve the opposite corner of the other panel in the same way. Separate the layers.

8 Press under ½" (1.3 cm) on the upper edge of the curtain. Then press under an amount equal to the rod-pocket depth plus the heading depth. If you are making a curtain panel with the ruffle beginning below the rod pocket, pin-mark the location of the lower stitching line for the rod pocket. Unfold the pressed edge.

9 Divide the ruffle strip into eighths, and pin-mark. Divide the curtain edge to be ruffled into eighths, beginning at the top of the heading or at the lower stitching line of the rod pocket and ending on the lower edge 3" (7.5 cm) from the raw edge on the return side of the panel. Pin the ruffle strip to the right side of the curtain, matching pin marks and raw edges.

10 Pull the gathering cord on the ruffle to fit the edge of the curtain. Ease in the fullness and pin the rest of the ruffle in place. Stitch the ruffle to the curtain a scant ½" (1.3 cm) from the raw edges.

11 Pin the lining to the curtain panel, right sides together, matching the raw edges on the ruffled side of the panel. Stitch a ½" (1.3 cm) seam on the ruffled edges.

12 Turn the curtain right side out, matching the remaining raw edges of the curtain and lining. Press the seam.

13 Press under 3" (7.5 cm) on the other side, folding the curtain and lining as one. Then unfold the pressed edge and turn the cut edge back, aligning it to the pressed fold line. Press the outer fold. Tack a drapery weight to the hem allowance, just above the lower edge. Refold the edge, forming a 1½" (3.8 cm) double-fold side hem. Stitch, using a blindstitch.

14 Finish the curtains as in steps 5 to 9 on page 48 for rod pocket curtains, treating the curtain and lining as one. Hang the curtains as on page 49. For curtains with two panels that meet in the middle, lap the ruffle that starts at the top of the heading over the shorter ruffle of the other panel.

Relaxed Rod-Pocket Curtains

*U*PDATED rod-pocket curtains have no heading ruffling above the rod. Relaxed rod-pocket curtains are also made with less fullness—sometimes no fullness—and the pockets are deep and loose instead of snug fitting. These contemporary curtains are often paired with sleek, narrow decorator rods for a casual look. Dress them up or down through your choice of fabric.

Soft touch (opposite)
Imagine this room without the curtains—much less soft and comfortable! Also, mounting the curtains high and puddling them on the floor visually raises the height of the ceiling and makes the room feel more spacious.

Casual elegance (top)
These silk curtains are interlined for plumpness and puddled onto the floor. Drawn back with rope-style tasseled tiebacks to reveal the contrasting lining, they enhance this gorgeous room.

Ultra-modern (left)
With clean, simple lines and up-to-the minute color, this room exudes confidence and class. The relaxed rod-pocket side panels on thin metal rods are so contemporary.

What you need to know

This curtain has no *heading*, only a *rod pocket*. The pocket should be very roomy, so the stitching line hangs 1" (2.5 cm) or more below the rod. Because rod-pocket styles are stationary by nature, they can be **designed** as separate panels hung at the sides of a window or as abutting panels that are parted and pulled back to the sides. One continuous panel can cover the window or be drawn to one side or to the center. For a casual or luxurious look, the curtains can be cut with 2" (5 cm) of extra length so the hem brushes the floor or with 12" to 15" (30.5 to 38 cm) of extra length for puddles. Another modern application is to hang flat rod-pocket panels on stationary rods or on rods that swing open or slide sideways on a track.

A single width of decorator fabric, gathered onto a rod at one-and-one-half to two times *fullness* will cover 32" to 24" (81.5 to 61 cm).

Choose **fabrics** that are very fluid and drapable, including sheer or semi-sheer fabrics. This style is often unlined, but you can line them and even interline (page 104) them for more body.

Choose a decorative rod and **mount** it before you cut the fabric, to be sure of accurate measurements. If the rod has finials and you don't want side *returns* on the curtains, extend the rod farther outside the window frame to minimize side light. Consider crane rods (page 118) for side treatments on curtains over doors or in-swinging windows.

Materials

- Decorative curtain rod
- Tools and hardware for installation
- Decorator fabric
- Drapery weights for floor-length curtains

Cutting directions

- The *cut length* of the fabric is equal to the finished length of the curtain plus the lower hem allowance (see chart on page 13) plus the depth of the rod pocket plus ½" (1.3 cm) for turn-under at the upper edge.

- The *cut width* of the fabric is equal to the amount of space you want to cover (including returns) multiplied by the desired fullness. Divide this amount by the width of the fabric and round up or down to the nearest whole or half width, to find the number of fabric widths you need. Use full or half widths of fabric for each curtain panel.

- Multiply the cut length by the total number of widths needed to determine the amount of fabric to buy. Buy an extra *pattern repeat* per fabric width for matching patterns (page 123).

Making relaxed rod-pocket curtains

1 Seam the fabric widths together, if necessary, for each curtain panel. If half widths are needed, add them at the sides of the panels. Finish the seam allowances together, and press them toward the side of the panel.

2 Press under the lower edge the full amount of the hem allowance. Then unfold the pressed edge and turn the cut edge back, aligning it to the pressed fold line. Press the outer fold. If you are making floor-length curtains with more than one fabric width, tack a drapery weight to the upper layer of fabric at the base of each seam, with the bottom of the weight near the inner fold.

3 Refold the lower edge, forming a double-fold hem, encasing the weights at the seams. Pin. Stitch, using a blindstitch for an invisible hem or a straight stitch for a visible hem.

4 Press under 3" (7.5 cm) on one side. Then unfold the pressed edge and turn the cut edge back, aligning it to the pressed fold line. Press the outer fold. Insert a drapery weight between the layers of the lower hem, and tack it in place. Refold the edge, forming a 1½" (3.8 cm) double-fold side hem. Stitch, using a blindstitch. Repeat for each side of each curtain panel.

5 Press under ½" (1.3 cm) at the upper edge. Then fold under the remaining rod-pocket allowance and pin; do not press a crease into the upper fold. Stitch close to the lower fold, forming the rod pocket.

6 Insert the rod through the pocket and mount the curtain. Distribute fullness evenly along the rod. Style the curtains as desired.

Stretched Curtains

CURTAINS STRETCHED taut from top to bottom over the window filter sunlight and provide privacy and softness. Often made of sheer or semisheer fabric, stretched curtains are a wonderful solution for French doors, door sidelights, and slim windows that do not open.

Filtered light (opposite)
Stretched rod-pocket curtains of pinstriped sheer fabric softly filter the light coming through French doors. Textured sheers dress up a window and look attractive from both sides.

Masking the view (top)
Lightweight stretched curtains on the lower halves of the windows let in light and provide privacy without blocking the view entirely. Double-hung windows like these can be opened from the top for air flow.

What you need to know

This **design** is a *rod-pocket* curtain with a pocket and *heading* on the bottom as well as the top. The headings should be only ½" to 1" (1.3 to 2.5 cm) deep, or they can be eliminated if you prefer. Stretched curtains are not suitable for casement or double-hung windows because the curtain fits tightly over the window from top to bottom. Stretched curtains can be used on door windows, sidelights, or in-swinging windows if the rods are attached directly to the window molding instead of the frame.

Use lightweight sheer or semisheer **fabrics**, including novelty sheers, casements, and laces. The curtains can be completely flat if you want a very sleek, contemporary look or if you want to show off a beautiful lace fabric. Otherwise use one-and-one-half to two times *fullness*.

Stretched curtains are **mounted** on narrow rods, called sash rods, at the top and bottom. These come with brackets that will hold the curtain the right distance from the glass. There are also spring-tension rods that can be used if the window frame is deep enough to accommodate them, thus eliminating the need to drill holes. When you install the rods, leave room at the top and bottom for a narrow heading, if you wish, or leave just enough room for the fabric gathered on the rod. Install the rods first so you can measure accurately for the curtains.

Materials

- Two sash rods or spring-tension rods
- Sheer or semisheer decorator fabric

Cutting directions

- The *cut length* is equal to the distance between rods, measured from the bottom of the top rod to the top of the bottom rod, plus four times the allowance for rod pocket and heading plus 1" (2.5 cm).

- The *cut width* is equal to the *finished width* multiplied by the desired fullness plus 4" (10 cm) for 1" (1.3 cm) double-fold side hems.

Making stretched curtains

1 Seam the fabric widths together, if necessary, using French seams in this manner: Place the panels wrong sides together. Stitch a scant ¼" (6 mm) seam. Press the seam allowances open. Turn the panels right sides together along the seam line, and stitch again ¼" (6 mm) from the edge, encasing the raw edges.

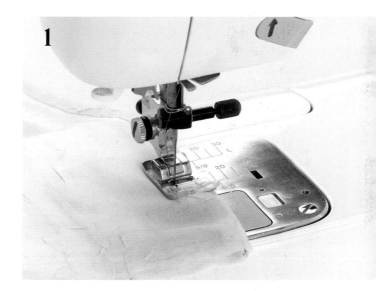

2 Press under 1" (2.5 cm) twice on the sides of the curtain panel; stitch to make double-fold hems, using a straight stitch or blindstitch.

3 Press under ½" (1.3 cm) on the upper edge. Then press under an amount equal to the rod-pocket depth plus the heading depth; pin.

4 Stitch close to the first fold. Stitch again at the depth of the heading.

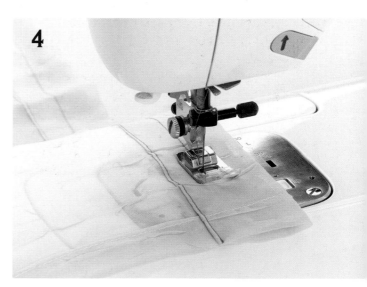

5 Repeat step 3 for the lower edge of the curtain panel.

6 Insert the rods through the rod pockets. Install the upper rod, then the lower rod. Adjust the fullness evenly.

Hourglass Curtains

*T*HESE GRACEFUL stretched curtains are cinched in at the "waistline." Often seen on French doors, they are also great for atrium doors and in-swinging windows or for sidelights and other narrow windows that do not open and close.

Dressing the view (opposite)
When privacy and light control aren't the issues, beautiful hourglass curtains like these entice you to take a closer, longer look at the doors and what lies beyond them. The sheer fabric filters light without hiding the door details.

Dressing the room (bottom)
The plaid hourglass curtains on these windows keep all the interest inside the room while letting in light at their sides. Jumbo cording covered with fabric is knotted attractively around each curtain. Though the matching door treatment is made to move with the door, the furniture arrangement suggests the homeowner rarely uses the door or opens the windows.

What you need to know

This is not just a stretched curtain (page 68) that is tied at the middle. The sides are made longer than the center so the curtain is equally taut in all areas. For this **design**, you need to take two length measurements, as shown on page 73.

Hourglass curtains are especially attractive in lace and sheer **fabrics**. They are often visible from both sides, so take that into consideration when selecting the fabric.

Mount the curtain with sash rods or other curtain rods with very shallow *projections* if the treatment is for a door. Use spring-tension rods for mounting the curtain inside a window frame. Install the rods and measure the window (opposite) before cutting the fabric.

Materials

- Two sash rods, curtain rods with up to 1¹/4" (3.2 cm) projection, or spring-tension rods
- Tools and hardware for installation
- Ribbon or twill tape for *mocking up* the shape
- Straightedge
- Sheer to lightweight decorator fabric
- White heavyweight sew-in interfacing

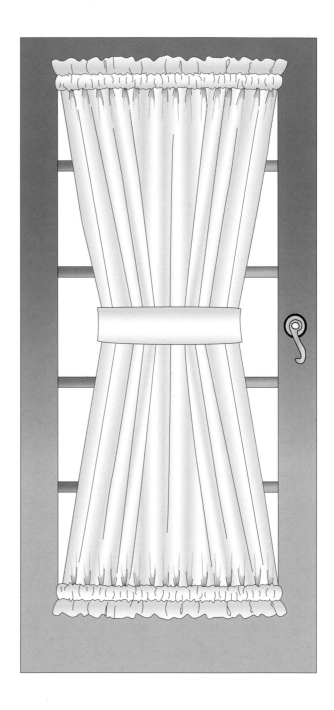

Measuring the window

1 Install the rods. Tape a strip of ribbon or twill tape to the door or window, outlining the desired shape of the curtain. Begin at the lower outside corner of the top rod, angling in the desired

distance to the center, and then out to the upper outside corner of the bottom rod. Repeat for the opposite side.

2 Measure the width of the curtain across the top or bottom; this is referred to as measurement 1. Measure the width of the curtain across the center; this is referred to as measurement 2. Subtract measurement 2 from measurement 1; record the difference.

3 Measure the length of the ribbon down one angled side; this is referred to as measurement 3. Measure the length of the curtain down the center, measuring from the lower edge of the top rod to the upper edge of the bottom rod; this is referred to as measurement 4. Subtract measurement 4 from measurement 3; record the difference.

Cutting directions

- The *cut length* of the fabric is equal to measurement 3 plus four times the rod-pocket depth and four times the desired heading depth plus 1" (2.5 cm) for turn-under.

- The *cut width* of the fabric is equal to measurement 1 multiplied by two to two-and-one-half times fullness plus 4" (10 cm) for 1" (2.5 cm) double-fold side hems.

- Cut a strip of fabric for the tieback, with the length equal to two times measurement 2 plus 1½" (3.8 cm) and the width equal to the desired finished width plus 1" (2.5 cm).

- Cut a strip of heavyweight sew-in interfacing 1" (2.5 cm) shorter than the cut length of the tieback strip and ⅛" (3 mm) narrower than the finished width of the tieback.

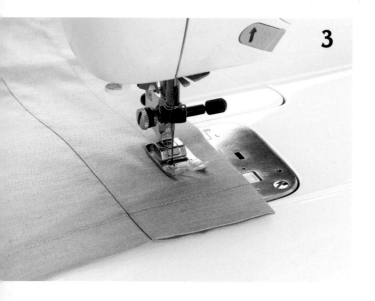

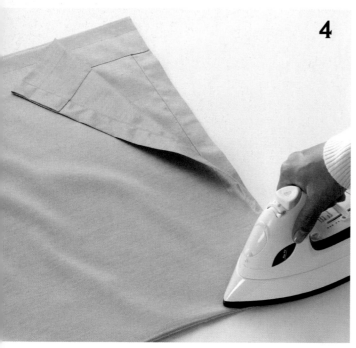

Making hourglass curtains

1 Seam the fabric widths together, if necessary, using French seams (page 69). Press under 1" (2.5 cm) twice on the sides of the curtain panel; stitch to make double-fold hems, using a straight stitch or blindstitch.

2 Press under ½" (1.3 cm) on the upper edge. Then press under an amount equal to the rod-pocket depth plus the heading depth; pin.

3 Stitch close to the first fold. Stitch again at the depth of the heading.

4 Repeat steps 2 and 3 for the lower edge of the curtain panel. Fold the curtain in half crosswise, right sides together, matching the top and the bottom rod pockets and headings. Press the fold line across the center of the curtain.

5 Divide the difference between measurement 1 and measurement 2 in half. Then multiply this number by the amount of fullness allowed for the curtain. Measure this distance along the pressed fold from one side toward the center; pin-mark. Repeat for the opposite side.

6 Divide the difference between measurement 3 and measurement 4 in half. Measure up from the fold at the pin marks a distance equal to this measurement; mark. Draw a line between the upper marks, parallel to the fold line.

7 Using a straightedge, extend the line to the pressed fold at the inner edges of the side hems, if sash rods or spring-tension rods are used. If the rods have up to a 1¼" (3.2 cm) projection, taper the line to 4" (10 cm) from the side hems. Stitch on the marked line, making a long dart.

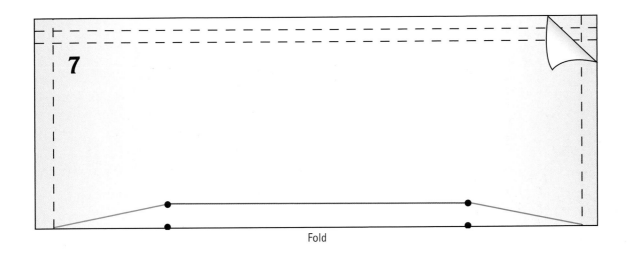

7

Fold

8 Press under ½" (1.3 cm) on one short end of the tieback. Fold the tieback in half lengthwise, right sides together; pin. Sew a ½" (1.3 cm) seam on the long edge; press the seam open.

9 Turn the tieback right side out, using a safety pin or bodkin. Center the seam on the back of the tieback; press. Insert the interfacing strip into the tieback.

10 Insert the unfinished end of the tieback into the pressed end, overlapping ½" (1.3 cm). Slipstitch the ends together, making a circular tieback.

11 Place the curtain through the tieback. Insert the spring-tension rods or sash rods in the top and bottom rod pockets. Mount the curtain, and check the fit.

12 Adjust the stitching of the dart, if necessary. Trim the fabric ½" (1.3 cm) from the stitched dart; finish the raw edges together, and press.

13 Reinstall the curtain. Secure the tieback to the center of the curtain, using a concealed safety pin.

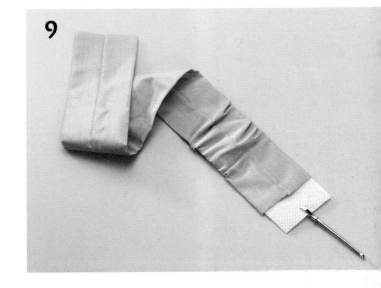

9

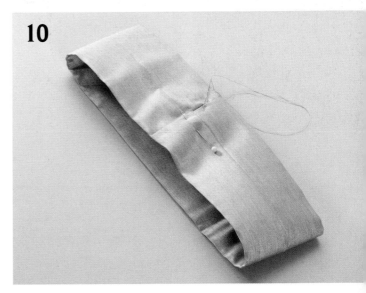

10

Tent-Flap Curtains

TRIM AND TAILORED tent-flap curtains are great for bedrooms, bathrooms, or home theaters where you want optimum light control and privacy. These flat panels attached to a mounting board are lined with decorative fabric because both sides show when the flaps are open. A great way to use two coordinating prints!

Partial view (opposite)
The curtain is drawn back for you—take a peek! This tent-flap curtain dresses a window with a deep ledge. A drapery holdback works as an attachment point for the curtain as well as a focal point. The simple styling is serene.

Tassel tabs (top)
Here's an innovative way to hang a simple lined rectangle of fabric. Tassel and medallion accents at the top also tie the tent flap to the pole. A matching cord medallion and tassel at the side anchor the flap.

Pretty frame (left)
What a pretty way to frame a window—and so simple, too. This tent-flap curtain is tailored and feminine all at once. The narrow ties at the sides can be purely decorative if you never intend to close the curtain, or make them workable if the room requires privacy and light control.

What you need to know

Tent-flap curtains work especially well for windows that are taller than they are wide. They can be **designed** in many ways. One panel can be drawn back from a corner or from partway up one side. Two slightly overlapping panels can be mounted side by side and drawn apart. Separate panels made to fit individual frames in a bank of windows can be drawn open in symmetrical or asymmetrical patterns. The flaps can be held open by slipping a buttonhole, grommet, or metal ring over a button or small wall hook.

Choose medium-weight, firmly woven decorator **fabrics** for both the front and lining. If the window receives strong light, avoid dark or bright colors for the lining because the curtain may fade noticeably. If you choose two print fabrics, layer them and hold them up to the light to see if the pattern from the back fabric shadows through to the front. You may need to *interline* them with plain drapery lining or black-out lining for maximum light control.

The curtains are attached to a 1 × 2 board for **mounting** and installed with angle irons. Cut the mounting board 2" (5 cm) wider than the window to allow room for the angle irons at the ends to fit just outside the window frame.

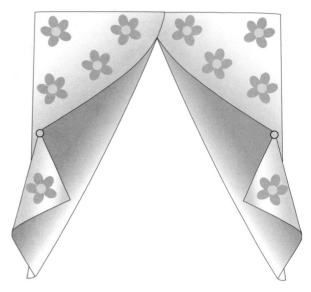

Cutting directions

- Cut one piece each of the two decorator fabrics for each curtain panel. The *cut length* of each panel is equal to the desired *finished length* plus the depth of the mounting board plus 1" (2.5 cm).

- For a curtain with two panels, the *cut width* of each panel is equal to one-half the width of the mounting board plus the depth of the mounting board plus 2" (5 cm). For a curtain with one panel, the cut width is equal to the width of the mounting board plus twice the depth of the board plus 1" (2.5 cm) for seam allowances.

- Cut a piece of drapery lining to the same size for each panel if interlining is necessary.

Making tent-flap curtains

1 Cover the mounting board with fabric (page 121). Attach angle irons at the ends, and mount the board above the window. Remove the board, leaving the angle irons on the wall.

Materials

- Mounting board
- Tools and hardware for installation
- Two different decorator fabrics
- Drapery lining, optional
- Staple gun and staples
- Findings for securing the curtain open, such as grommets, metal rings, buttons, wall hooks, cup hooks, or Velcro
- Self-adhesive Velcro

3

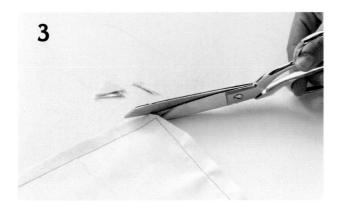

4

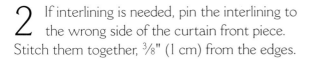

5

2 If interlining is needed, pin the interlining to the wrong side of the curtain front piece. Stitch them together, ⅜" (1 cm) from the edges.

3 Pin the front to the back, wrong sides together, matching raw edges. Stitch ½" (1.3 cm) seams on all sides, leaving an opening at the top for turning. Trim seam allowances diagonally at the corners.

4 Press the seam allowances open. Turn the panel right side out. Press the edges, pressing in the seam allowances at the opening.

5 Repeat steps 2 to 4 for any additional panels. Hold the panels up to the window to decide on the best position for holding the curtains open. Mark the locations for buttons, grommets, or rings. Stitch buttonholes, insert a grommets, or hand-stitch metal rings at the marks.

6

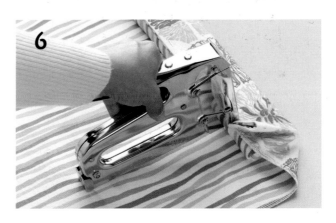

6 Center the panels on the mounting board, aligning the upper edges to the board back and wrapping the sides around the board ends. The panels will overlap 1" (2.5 cm) at the center. Staple the panels to the board, mitering the corners.

7 Install the curtain above the window, re-attaching the board to the angle irons. Attach the desired findings to the curtain and wall for holding the curtain open.

8

8 Cut two blocks of 1 × 2 board. Secure an angle iron to the narrow edge of each block, and attach one block on each side of the window frame at the height of the button. Secure the panel to the wood with self-adhesive Velcro.

Pinch-Pleated Draperies

CLASSIC PLEATED DRAPERIES are the ultimate window treatment for versatility and style. Installed on traverse rods, they easily open to reveal the full window view. When closed, they offer privacy, light control, and even insulation. They can also be made as stationary draperies. Traditional threefold pinch pleats will create uniform, graceful folds.

Tall and tasteful (opposite)

Perfectly styled pinch pleats, mounted at ceiling level for extra height and drama, afford full access to the doors, yet can be closed completely when needed. With their small-scale geometric pattern and rich, buttery color, these draperies provide a tasteful background for the room's furnishings.

Stately elegance (top)

Floor-to-ceiling draperies work well in this sunny atrium. They draw attention to the impressive ceiling and offer a break from the expanse of white woodwork and glass. Tied low with hefty cord and tassel tiebacks and spilling onto the marble floor, these stationary treatments add to the stately elegance of the room.

Unifying solution (bottom)

The different size doors and windows in this bedroom posed a decorating problem solved by the pinch-pleated, traversing draperies. Though there are shades over the glass to filter light and give privacy, closing the draperies also darkens and warms the room. The light fabric color that contrasts with the walls moves the eye around the room.

What you need to know

The instructions that follow are for a pair of drapery panels mounted on a two-way-draw traverse rod. When **designing** the treatment, allow for the *stacking space* at the sides of the window so the draperies will clear the window when they are open. The actual stacking space varies, depending on the weight of the fabric, the fullness of the draperies, and whether or not they are lined but is estimated at one-third the width of the windows; allow for one-half of the stacking space on each side of the window.

A wide range of decorator **fabrics** can be used, including sheers, casements, semisheers, and medium-weight fabrics in both prints and solids. Two-and-one-half times fullness is used for most draperies, but for sheers, three times fullness can be used. For lace draperies, use two-and-one-half times fullness so the pattern of the lace is noticeable in the finished draperies.

After you measure the window and determine the stacking space, purchase the rod and **mount** it on the wall above and to the outside of the window frame. If the draperies will hang from a conventional traverse rod, measure for the finished length from the top of the rod to where you want the lower edge of the draperies; then add ½" (1.3 cm) so the draperies will extend above the rod. If the draperies will hang from a decorative rod, measure from the bottom of the rod to the desired finished length. If the draperies will hang from a pole set with rings, measure from the pin holes in the rings to the desired finished length.

Materials

- Conventional or decorative traverse rod
- Tools and hardware for installation
- Decorator fabric
- Drapery weights
- Drapery lining for lined curtains
- *Buckram*, 4" (10 cm) wide
- Drapery hooks

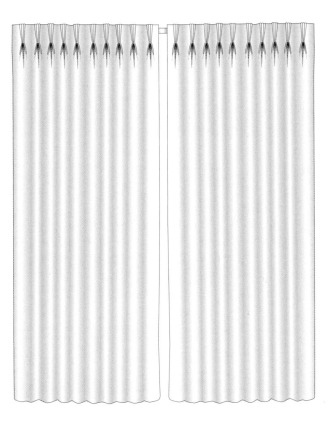

Cutting directions

- Use the Fabric Worksheet (page 83) to find the necessary measurements. Several widths of fabric are often required. Cut the number of fabric widths you need to the calculated *cut length* of the draperies.

Making unlined pinch-pleated draperies

1 Seam the fabric widths together as necessary. If half widths are needed, add them at the sides of the panels. Finish the seams together, and press them toward the side of the panel.

2 Press under the lower edge 8" (20.5 cm) for the hem. Then unfold the pressed edge and turn the cut edge back, aligning it to the pressed fold line. Press the outer fold. If the panel has more than one fabric width, tack a drapery weight to the upper layer of fabric at the base of each seam, with the bottom of the weight near the inner fold.

3 Refold the lower edge, forming a 4" (10 cm) double-fold hem, encasing the weights at the seams. Pin. Stitch, using a blindstitch for an invisible hem or a straight stitch for a visible hem.

4 Press under the upper edge 8" (20.5 cm). Then unfold the pressed edge and turn the cut edge back, aligning it to the pressed fold line. Press the outer fold. Cut buckram the width of each drapery panel. Slip the buckram under the first fold, and then refold the top, encasing the buckram. Pin in place.

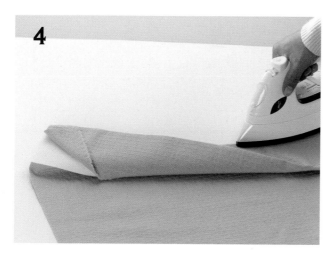

DRAPERY FABRIC WORKSHEET

Drapery length

Desired *finished length*

+ 8" (20.5 cm) for heading

+ 8" (20.5 cm) for 4" (10 cm) double-fold lower hem

= *cut length* of drapery *

*If you buy fabric with a *pattern repeat*, your cut length must be rounded up to the next number evenly divisible by the pattern repeat.

Drapery width

Rod width (from end bracket to end bracket on conventional rods; from end ring to end ring on decorative rods)

+ allowance for two *returns* [*projection* of rod plus $\frac{1}{2}$" (1.3 cm) for each return]

+ $3\frac{1}{2}$" (9 cm) for overlap

= *finished width* of drapery

Total number of drapery fabric widths

Finished drapery width

× multiplied by $2\frac{1}{2}$ to 3 times *fullness*

÷ divided by width of fabric

= total number of fabric widths needed, rounded up or down to nearest full width

Number of fabric widths per panel

Total number of fabric widths

÷ divided by 2

= number of fabric widths per panel

Amount to purchase

Total number of fabric widths

× multiplied by cut length

= amount to purchase

LINING FABRIC WORKSHEET

Lining length

Cut length of drapery

− 5" (12.7 cm)

= cut length of lining

Number of lining widths

Same as for total number of drapery fabric widths (above).

Lining fabric width must be the same as the decorator fabric width.

PLEATS WORKSHEET

Finished panel width

Finished drapery width (see chart on page 83)

÷ divided by 2

= finished panel width

Number of pleats per panel

Number of drapery fabric widths per panel (see chart on page 83)

× multiplied by number of pleats per width*

= number of pleats per panel

Space between pleats

Finished panel width (see chart on page 83)

- overlap and return

= width to be pleated

÷ divided by number of spaces per panel (one less than number of pleats per panel)

= space between pleats

Pleat size

Flat width of hemmed panel

- finished panel width (figured above)

= total amount allowed for pleats

÷ divided by number of pleats per panel (figured above)

= pleat size

* Plan 5 pleats per width of 48" (122 cm) fabric, 6 pleats per width of 54" (137 cm) fabric. For example, for 54" (137 cm) fabric, 3 widths per panel = 18 pleats. If you have a half width of fabric, plan 2 or 3 pleats in that half width.

5 Press under 3" (7.5 cm) on one side. Then unfold the pressed edge and turn the cut edge back, aligning it to the pressed fold line. Press the outer fold. Insert a drapery weight between the layers of the lower hem, and tack it in place. Refold the edge, forming a 1½" (3.8 cm) double-fold side hem. Stitch. Repeat for each side of each curtain panel.

6 Determine the number and size of pleats and spaces between them by working through the chart below. The recommended amount of fabric for each pleat is 4" to 6" (10 to 15 cm). The recommended space between pleats is 3½" to 4" (9 to 10 cm). If the calculation from the worksheets results in pleats or spaces that are greater than the amount recommended, add one more pleat and space. If the calculation results in pleats or spaces smaller than the amount recommended, subtract one pleat and space.

7 Cut buckram templates in sizes to match the determined pleats and spaces; cut five of each for 48" (122 cm) fabric or six of each for 54" (137 cm) fabric. Mark the overlap and return on the right side of one panel, using chalk. Arrange the templates on the first fabric width, with the first pleat starting at the overlap line and the last pleat ending at the seam line. There will be one less space. Adjust the pleat sizes to arrange the spaces evenly; spaces must remain uniform. Mark the heading even with the outer edges of the space templates.

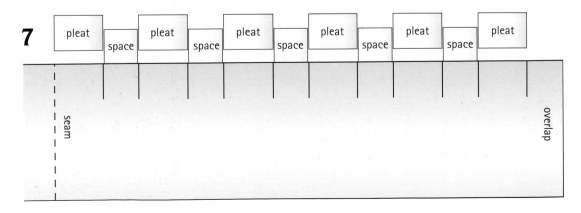

8 | pleat | space | pleat | space | pleat | space | pleat | space | pleat | space | pleat | space |

return

seam

8 Arrange the templates on the second fabric width from the overlap, with the first space starting at the first seam line from the overlap and the last pleat ending at the next seam line; use the same number of pleats as spaces. Repeat for each panel. (The last pleat ends at the return mark in the last fabric width.) Adjust the pleats as necessary; mark the spaces. If the return end of the panel has a half width of fabric, plan for two pleats if the fabric is 48" (122 cm) wide or for three pleats if the fabric is 54" (137 cm) wide. Transfer the markings to the opposite panel in mirror-image placement.

9 Fold each pleat by bringing the pleat lines together; pin. Crease the buckram on the fold.

10 Stitch on the pleat line from the top of the heading to the lower edge of the buckram; backstitch to secure. Repeat for each pleat in each panel.

11 Check the finished width of the panel along the heading. Adjust the size of a few pleats if necessary to adjust the width of the panel.

12 To divide each stitched pleat into three even pleats, grasp the center crease and push it down toward the stitching line, forcing the sides to spread out. Form the fabric into three even pleats and press creases in the buckram with your fingers.

(continued)

10

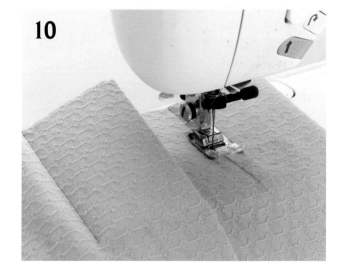

12

13 Bar-tack pleats by machine just above the lower edge of the buckram; or tack pleats by hand, using a stabstitch and heavy-duty thimble.

Hanging and dressing the draperies

1 Insert drapery hooks, with one hook at each pleat and one hook near each end of the panel. On a conventional traverse rod, the top of the hook is 1¾" (4.5 cm) from the upper edge of the overdrapery or 1¼" (3.2 cm) from the upper edge of the underdrapery. On a pole set with rings, the top of the hook is ¼" (6 mm) from the upper edge. On a decorator traverse rod, the top of the hook is ¾" to 1" (2 to 2.5 cm) from the upper edge.

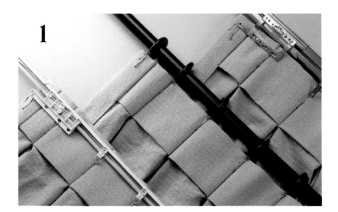

2 Crease the buckram midway between each pleat; fold it forward if a conventional traverse rod is being used, or fold it to the back if a decorative traverse rod is being used. This is often referred to as "cracking" the buckram. After cracking the buckram, press the draperies, using a warm, dry iron.

3 Hang the end hook at the return in the hole on the side of the bracket. Hang the hook of the first pleat in the hole at the front corner of the bracket.

4 Hang the hooks for middle pleats on the slides; remove any slides that are not used. Hang the hook for the last pleat in the first hole of the master slide. Hang the end hook on the overlap of the drapery in the end hole of the master slide. Pinch the hooks on the master slides closed to keep them from catching when the draperies are drawn; also, pull the front master slide slightly forward, if necessary.

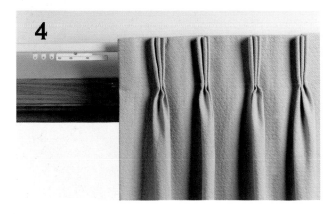

5 Open the draperies completely into the stacked position. Check the heading to be sure the buckram is folded as it was cracked in step 2. Starting at the heading, guide the pleats into evenly spaced soft folds of equal depth; follow the grain line of the fabric to keep the pleats perpendicular to the floor.

6 Staple a narrow strip of matching fabric or muslin around the drapery panel, midway between the heading and hem, to hold the pleats in place. Avoid pulling the fabric too tightly or you will create unwanted wrinkles.

7 Staple a second strip of fabric at the hemline. Check to see that the draperies hang straight down from the rod. Leave the draperies in this position for two weeks to set the pleats. In humid conditions, one week may be sufficient.

Making lined pleated draperies

1 Prepare the drapery panels as in steps 1 to 3 on page 83. Repeat for the lining panels, making 2" (5 cm) double-fold lower hems and omitting weights.

2 Place the drapery panel on a large flat surface. Lay the lining panel on top of the drapery panel, wrong sides together, with the lower edge of the lining 1" (2.5 cm) above the lower edge of the drapery panel; raw edges should be even at the sides.

3 Mark the lining panel 8" (20.5 cm) from the upper edge of the drapery panel. Trim on the marked line. This will be even with the top fold of the heading.

4 Finish the draperies as in steps 4 to 13 on pages 83 to 86, treating the decorator fabric and lining as one. The lining will be caught in the stitches of the pleats and in the side hems.

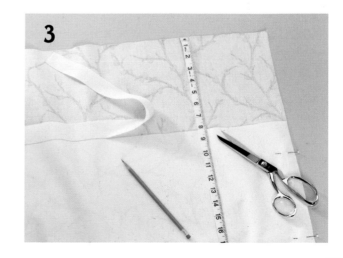

3

Pleat Alternatives

G O BEYOND the classic pinch pleat with these variations that really add a designer touch. Options for creative drapery headings include goblet pleats, fan pleats, butterfly pleats, inverted pinch pleats, and cartridge pleats.

Fringed cartridge pleats (opposite)
The heading of this cartridge-pleat drapery is stitched into cylinders that extend into the body of the drapery as soft, rounded folds. Cleverly placed wide fringe trim calls attention to the heading and changes the drapery from a quiet backdrop to an energizing room accent.

Fan pleats (top)
Also called Euro pleats or Parisian pleats, fan pleats are pinch pleats that are tacked at the top. They fan downward into soft, rolling folds that have a more contemporary look. This is a very popular style.

Silk goblets (left)
Open tubes that are pinched into pleats at the bottom resemble wine glasses—thus the name "goblet pleats." Shown here in a silky, yellow, giant plaid fabric, goblet pleats give the draperies a dressed-up look. For added detailing, the base of each goblet is often embellished with a covered button.

What you need to know

Design the draperies following the guidelines and worksheets for pinch-pleated draperies (page 83). The only difference here is the method and style of pleating, which is the last phase of the construction.

• Goblet pleats are similar to three-fold pinch pleats at the base, but the tops are belled out to resemble wine glasses.

• Fan pleats (also called Euro pleats) are pinch pleated with the tacking done at the top instead of the base.

• Butterfly pleats can have two or three folds with tacking done about 1" (2.5 cm) above the base. The folds are drawn to the sides and tacked at the top of the heading to resemble wings.

• Inverted pinch pleats are just like standard pinch pleats, only the pleat is formed on the back of the heading.

• Cartridge pleats are tubular; they are not divided into folds.

To draw attention to the pleats, you can add dressmaker detailing, such as covered buttons at the base of goblet pleats or a decorative trim along the base of cartridge pleats.

Choose lightweight or medium-weight decorator **fabrics** for any of these styles. The draperies can be lined and interlined, depending on the look you want.

Mount the drapery hardware, following the same guidelines for pinch-pleated draperies. With the exception of inverted pinch pleats, any of the pleat styles can be hung from conventional traverse rods or decorative rods. Because of the bulk on the back of the heading, avoid conventional traverse rods for inverted pinch pleats.

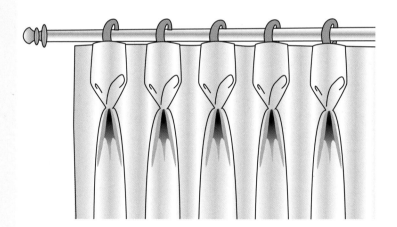

Making goblet pleats

1 Follow the charts and directions for making pinch-pleated draperies on pages 83 to 86, up through step 11, but do not crease the buckram in step 9.

2 Pinch the fabric at the bottom of the buckram into three or four small pleats. Tack the pleats by hand, using a stabstitch and heavy-duty thimble; or bar-tack the pleats by machine just above the lower edge of the buckram.

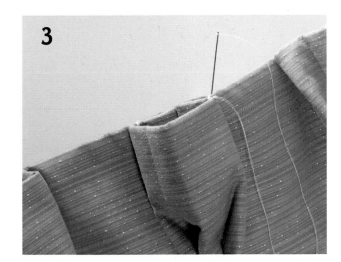

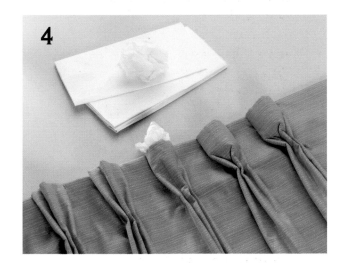

3　Form each pleat into a rounded, goblet shape. Hand-stitch the pleat along the upper edge of the drapery, up to ½" (1.3 cm) on each side of the stitching line.

4　Insert wadded tissue paper or sections of foam pipe insulation into the pleats to help them retain the shape.

5　Hang and dress the draperies as on pages 86 and 87.

Making fan pleats

1　Follow the charts and directions for making pinch-pleated draperies on pages 83 to 85, up through step 11.

2　At the top of each pleat, form the fabric into three even pleats and press creases in the buckram with your fingers.

3　Bar-tack the pleats by machine near the top of the curtain; or tack pleats by hand, using a

(continued)

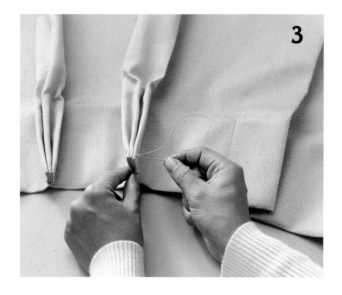

stabstitch and heavy-duty thimble. The pleats will fan outward from the top.

4 Hang and dress the draperies as on pages 86 and 87.

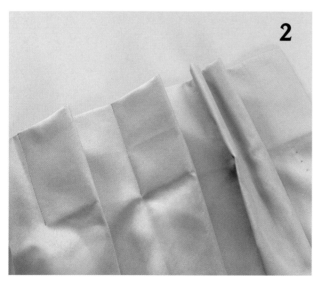

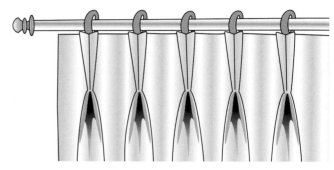

Making butterfly pleats

1 Follow the charts and directions for making pinch-pleated draperies on pages 83 to 86, up through step 11.

2 Push the center of each pleat down over the pleat stitching line, forcing the sides outward. Then form the sides into two even pleats.

3 Bar-tack the pleats by machine 1" (2.5 cm) above the lower edge of the buckram; or tack pleats by hand, using a stabstitch and heavy-duty thimble.

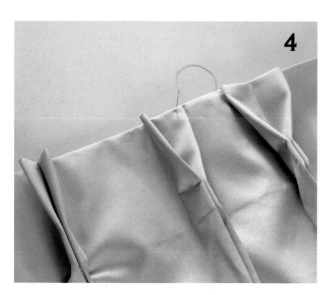

4 Turn the pleats to the sides at the top and hand-stitch them to the heading. The pleats will fan out above and below the tack, like the wings of a butterfly.

5 Hang and dress the draperies as on pages 86 and 87.

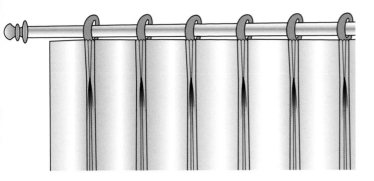

Making inverted pinch pleats

1 Follow the charts and directions for making pinch-pleated draperies on pages 83 to 85, up through step 8. In steps 7 and 8, make the marks on the wrong side of the heading.

2 Follow steps 9 to 13, pages 85 and 86, but fold the pleats to the back side of the heading.

3 Hang and dress the draperies as on pages 86 and 87.

2

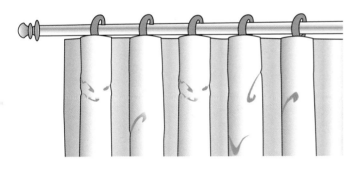

Making cartridge pleats

1 Follow the charts and directions for making pinch-pleated draperies on pages 83 to 86, up through step 11. You'll probably want the pleats closer, so plan on one more pleat per fabric width and half width. In step 9, don't crease the buckram.

2 To hold the shape of the cartridge pleats, insert a section of foam pipe insulation into each pleat.

3 Hang and dress the draperies as on pages 86 and 87.

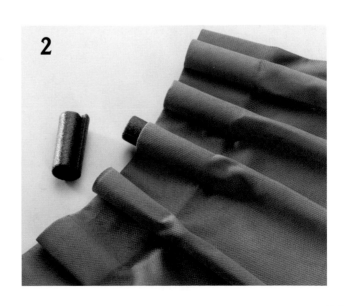

2

Inverted Box-Pleat Draperies

BOX PLEATS have long been used for valances, dust ruffles, or skirts on upholstered furniture; now they're popular for full-length draperies as well. In an inverted pleat, the fullness is folded out to the back of the heading, creating a smooth line on the front, perfect for a tailored, modern look.

Modern tailoring (opposite)
Color-blocked panels in red and taupe provide a colorful solution for this family room patio door. The inverted box pleats at the drapery heading reflect the modern tone of the room.

Quietly tasteful (top)
A classy treatment for a bank of windows, these inverted box-pleat drapery panels are stationary layers over traversing sheer pinch-pleat draperies. In an ivory color that melds with the wallcovering, they are understated and lovely.

Beaded accent (right)
A closer look reveals the beaded trim that accents the box-pleat heading and dresses up the drapery panels like a string of pearls at a neckline.

What you need to know

Follow the guidelines and worksheets for pinch-pleated draperies (pages 83 to 86). **Design** these draperies with two-and-one-half to three times *fullness*. The more fullness in the pleats, the more cumbersome the draperies will be to stack back, so if they are meant to traverse, use less fullness. This style is often used as elegant side panels or as single panels on a narrow window, drawn to one side with a tieback or holdback.

Medium-weight decorator **fabrics** work best, though you can beef up an elegant lightweight silk fabric with flannel interlining for a truly posh look. Because of its sleek lines, this drapery style is a good candidate for banding along the sides and bottom or for added details, such as buttons or decorator trims at the heading.

Follow the same guidelines for **mounting** the rod as for other draperies (page 118). Avoid conventional traverse rods, as the added bulk on the back of the heading will make it difficult to draw the draperies.

Materials

- Decorative rod or conventional rod
- Tools and hardware for installation
- Decorator fabric
- Lining
- Interlining, optional
- *Buckram*
- Drapery weights
- Drapery hooks or sew-on or clip-on rings

Making inverted box-pleat draperies

1 If interlined, follow cutting directions and steps for interlined draperies, page 103, to prepare the panels. If not interlined, follow the cutting directions and steps for lined draperies on page 87.

2 Calculate the pleat and space sizes, using the chart on page 83. Plan four pleats per width of 48" (122 cm) fabric, five pleats per width of 54" (137 cm) fabric, two pleats in any half widths.

3 Cut templates in sizes to match the pleats and spaces. Mark the overlap and return on the wrong side of one panel, using chalk. Arrange the templates on the first fabric width, with the first pleat starting at the overlap line and the last pleat spanning the seam. There will be one less space. Adjust the pleat sizes to arrange the spaces evenly; spaces must remain uniform. Mark the heading even with the outer edges of the space templates.

4 Arrange the templates on the second fabric width from the overlap, with the first space abutting the last pleat of the first panel and the last pleat incorporating the next seam line; use the same number of pleats as spaces. Repeat for each panel. (The last pleat ends at the return mark in the last fabric width.) Adjust the pleats as necessary; mark the spaces. Transfer the markings to the opposite panel in mirror-image placement.

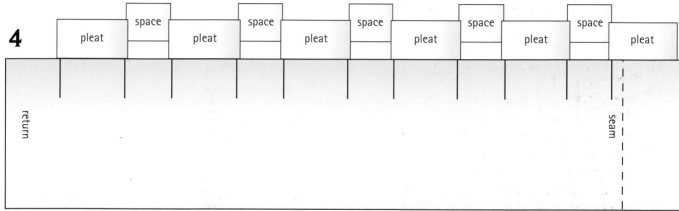

3

| pleat | space | pleat | space | pleat | space | pleat | space | pleat |

-seam

overlap

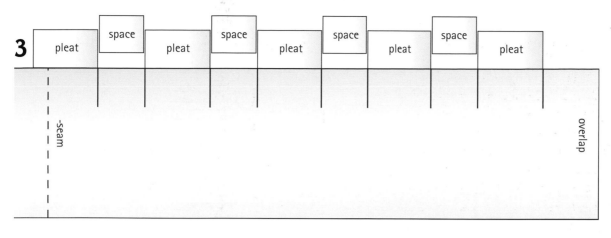

4

| pleat | space | pleat | space | pleat | space | pleat | space | pleat | space | pleat |

return

seam

5 Fold each pleat to the back of the heading by bringing the pleat lines together; pin. Stitch on the pleat line from the top of the heading to the lower edge of the buckram; backstitch to secure.

6 Check the finished width of the panel along the heading. Adjust the size of a few pleats, if necessary, to adjust the width of the panel.

7 Flatten each pleat, distributing the fullness evenly to the sides. Stitch in the ditch of the pleat seam from the right side to keep the pleat flat against the back of the heading.

8 Insert a drapery hook into the back of the heading next to the center stitching line of each pleat. Or attach sew-on or clip-on rings at the center of each pleat. Hang the drapery.

5

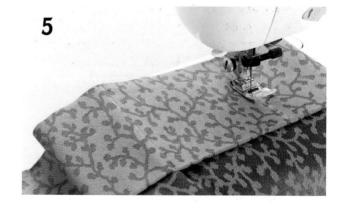

8

Banded Treatments

BANDING DEFINES the edges of a curtain or drapery. A solid-color band can accent a patterned panel, giving visual weight to the sides and anchoring the lower edge. A patterned band can add excitement to otherwise plain draperies while connecting them to the room's decor. A versatile design addition, banding is suitable for many styles of window treatments.

Formal in brocade (opposite)
Brocade curtains, detailed with banding and tassel trim, provide an elegant backdrop for this formal sitting room. Extra fullness is shaped into deep, even folds. Hidden wands make it easy to close the curtains for privacy.

Bias banding (top)
What a clever way to turn a hole-in-the wall window into an attractive room feature. This sweet, simple treatment—a combination tab (page 29) and tent-flap (page 77)—is subtly edged with reversible banding cut on the *bias*.

Well defined (left)
Inverted box-pleat draperies (page 95) with contrast banding dress the corner windows in this graceful, tailored living room. Just as the dark wood of the chairs defines the upholstered seats and backs, the drapery banding defines its borders.

$\mathcal{W}$hat you need to know

In this **design**, faced banding is applied to the sides and lower edge of the window treatment, eliminating the need for side and bottom hems. For a professional finish, the corners are mitered. The width of the banding is a matter of personal taste. To help you decide, *mock up* some samples at the window and stand back to choose which one you like best. Banding can be added to lots of curtain styles, including flat panel, tab, or rod-pocket as well as pleated draperies. Since the heading (or top) of the treatment is usually finished last, simply follow the directions for the banding and complete the treatment following the directions for the style you choose.

Banding is suitable for treatments made from medium-weight, lightweight, or even sheer **fabrics**, offering stability to the edges as well as a decorative effect. For best results, the banding fabric should be a stable, opaque fabric. Whenever possible, cut the banding strips on the lengthwise grain of the fabric, eliminating or minimizing the need for distracting seams in the banding.

Follow the guidelines for **mounting** the treatment that are included with the style you choose.

Cutting directions

- To determine the *cut length*, follow the cutting directions for the curtain or drapery style you choose, but allow only ½" (1.3 cm) for a lower seam allowance instead of the usual lower hem allowance.

- To determine the *cut width*, follow the cutting directions for the curtain or drapery style you

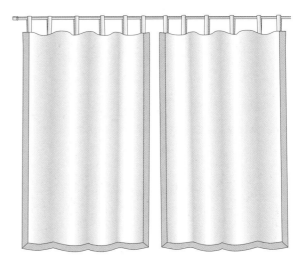

choose, but allow only ½" (1.3 cm) for a side seam allowances instead of the usual side hem allowances.

- Cut banding strips ½" (1.3 cm) longer than the cut length or cut width of each edge to be banded and 1" (2.5 cm) wider than the desired finished width of the band.

- If lining is desired, cut the lining pieces to the same size as the curtain or drapery pieces.

Making unlined banded treatments

1 Seam the fabric widths together as necessary for each curtain panel, adding any half widths at the *return* ends of the panels. Finish the seam allowances together, and press them toward the side of the panel.

2 Press under ½" (1.3 cm) along one long edge of each banding strip. Mark a point ½" (1.3 cm) from the end of the strip, ½" (1.3 cm) from the unpressed edge. Repeat for all the strips.

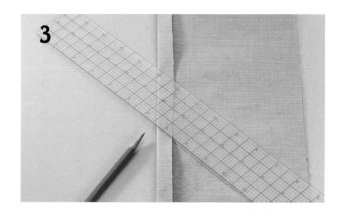

3 Pin the ends of adjoining strips right sides together, matching the pressed edges and raw edges. Draw a line from the marked point to the pressed edge at a 45-degree angle.

4 Stitch along the line through the marked point to the outer corner. Trim the seam allowance to ¼" (6 mm). Press the seam allowances open. Repeat for each set of adjoining strips to miter the corners.

5 Pin the banding strip, right side out, to the right side of the curtain, matching raw edges. Pin the band facing over the band, right sides together, matching raw edges and mitered seams.

6 Stitch ½" (1.3 cm) from the raw edges through all layers. Pivot the stitching at the mitered seams.

7 Trim the seam allowances diagonally across the corners. Fold out the facing strip, and press the seam open between the band and facing, getting as close as possible to the corners.

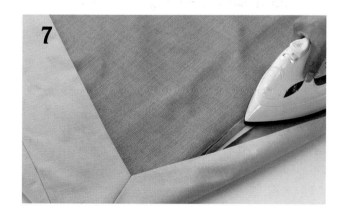

8 Turn the facing to the back of the curtain. Press along the seam. Glue-baste or pin the banding and facing strips in place along the inner pressed edges.

9 Topstitch along the inner edge of the band, catching the inner edge of the facing on the back of the treatment.

10 Finish the top of the curtain or drapery following the directions for the desired style. Treat the band and fabric as one.

Making lined banded treatments

1 Follow step 1, opposite, for the curtain or drapery panels and for the lining panels. Pin or baste the pieces wrong sides together.

2 Finish the treatment as in steps 2 to 10, treating the decorator fabric and lining as one.

Interlined Treatments

THE SECRET to an opulent look in curtains or draperies is a flannel interlining. It is a must with decorator silks, which would look limp and skimpy otherwise, but it also gives other fabrics a body-building boost. The insulating quality of the interlining also helps protect the fabric from sunlight. Once available only to the professional workroom, drapery interlining is now sold in fabric stores.

Pinstripes and tassels (opposite)
Salmon pinstripe silk, sewn into a relaxed rod-pocket curtain, is given extra body and volume with invisible flannel interlining. Trimmed with tassel fringe and flipped casually behind a metal holdback, this is a lush window treatment.

Lavish layers (top)
Muted earth tones and a lavishly layered window treatment are soothing and cozy in this bedroom. The interlined rod-pocket curtain, trimmed with tassel fringe, is pulled back to reveal the contrasting lining.

Crumpled silk (right)
Interlining exaggerates the wonderfully scrunched look of these silk draperies. Installed just under the molding and wall-to-wall across a bay of windows, the draperies soften the room corners and emphasize the high ceiling. To make it easier to manipulate the extra bulk, these pinch pleats have two folds instead of three.

What you need to know

The directions that follow are for any style of pleated draperies, though interlining can also be used to boost the volume of other treatments, including relaxed rod-pocket curtains and styling tape curtains. **Design** your treatment using the guidelines and worksheets for pinch-pleated draperies (pages 83 to 86). To emphasize the beefed-up look, draperies are often made extra long to brush the floor, puddle on the floor, or billow over tiebacks.

Use interlining with any **fabric** when you want to make it appear more billowy. Lightweight fabrics, especially decorator silks, really benefit from the use of interlining.

When choosing hardware and **mounting** it on the wall, follow the guidelines for the treatment style. Because the interlining will add more weight to your draperies, be sure to use enough brackets for the rod and install them into wall studs or use molly bolts (page 119).

Materials

- Decorative curtain rod
- Tools and hardware for installation
- Decorator fabric
- Drapery weights for floor-length curtains
- Flannel drapery interlining
- Drapery lining
- *Buckram*, 4" (10 cm) wide
- Drapery hooks

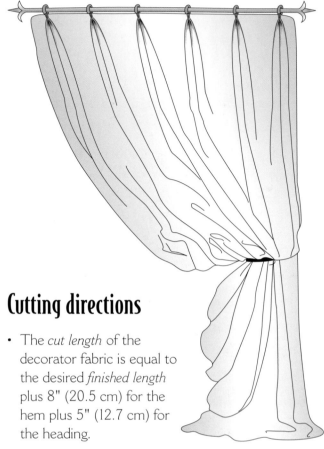

Cutting directions

- The *cut length* of the decorator fabric is equal to the desired *finished length* plus 8" (20.5 cm) for the hem plus 5" (12.7 cm) for the heading.

- The cut length of the lining is equal to the desired finished length of the drapery plus 4" (10 cm) for the hem plus 5" (12.7 cm) for the heading.

- The cut length of the interlining is equal to the desired finished length of the drapery plus 2" (5 cm) for the hem plus 5" (12.7 cm) for the heading.

- Follow the same guidelines for width as for pleated draperies.

Making interlined draperies

1. Follow steps 1 to 3 for pinch-pleated draperies on page 83. Repeat for the lining panels, making 2" (5 cm) double-fold lower hems and omitting weights. Repeat for the interlining, making 1" (2.5 cm) double-fold lower hems and omitting weights.

2. Place the lining right side up on a large flat surface. Place the drapery panel, right side down over the lining, aligning the tops of the hems. Place

the interlining over the drapery panel, right side up, aligning the tops of the hems. The lining will be 1½" (3.8 cm) shorter than the drapery, and the interlining will be 3" (7.5 cm) shorter than the drapery.

3 Measure from the bottom of the drapery panel a length equal to the finished length plus the width of the buckram plus ½" (1.3 cm), and mark a line. Cut off excess fabric of all three layers evenly on the marked line.

4 Pin the buckram over the three layers, even with the upper edge. Stitch through the buckram and all three layers ¼" (6 mm) from the lower edge of the buckram.

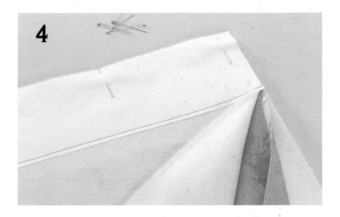

5 Turn the drapery right side out. At the top, there will be ¼" (6 mm) of the decorator fabric showing above the lining on the back of the drapery. Press the heading over a padded surface to avoid imprinting the seam allowances onto the front.

6 Press under 3" (7.5 cm) on one side, treating all three layers as one. Then unfold the pressed edge and turn the cut edge back, aligning it to the pressed fold line. Press the outer fold. To reduce bulk at the bottom hem, cut away the interlining up to the inner fold; cut away the lining up to the outer fold. Insert a drapery weight between the layers of the decorator fabric hem, and tack it in place.

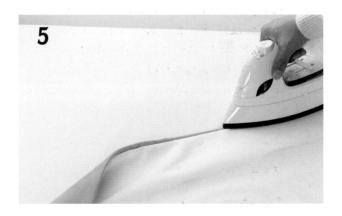

7 Refold the edge, forming a 1½" (3.8 cm) double-fold side hem. Repeat for each side of each curtain panel. Blindstitch the side hems from the base of the heading to the top of the bottom hem, leaving long tails of thread at the beginning and end. Using the thread tails, finish stitching the hems by hand.

8 Pleat the heading as desired, beginning with step 6 on page 84 for pinch-pleated draperies, or following the directions for one of the pleat variations on page 89, or following the directions for inverted box pleats on page 96.

Treatments with Attached Valances

GET THE LAYERED LOOK with a curtain and valance all in one. This stationary treatment is perfect as side panels over another treatment like pleated shades or blinds, when you don't want to build an additional layer with a valance on another rod. Vary the look with the heading style of your choice.

Formal gathering (opposite)
Full rod-pocket side panels frame the window behind the sofa in this formal living room. Mounted at ceiling height and drawn back very low, these curtains with attached valances are very elegant and sophisticated.

Buttoned goblets (top)
Goblet pleats accented with covered buttons top off the attached valance on side panel draperies. Contrast banding and glass bead fringe define the angled lower edge of the valance, transforming a minimal treatment into a dynamic statement.

Flat-panel plus (left)
Beefed up with interlining and topped with a jaunty plaid attached valance, this flat-panel silk curtain is anything but flat. Bullion fringe at the bottom of the valance adds even more elegance.

What you need to know

Attached valances can be **designed** as two separate curtain panels, each with its own valance, hanging at the sides of the window. Two pulled-back panels can meet in the center of the window and share one attached valance. The top can be pleated in one of the pleat styles on pages 89 to 95. It can also be pleated or gathered, using styling tape as on page 41, or it can have a *rod pocket* with or without a *heading*. Banding, fringe, or decorator trim along the lower edge of the valance will help separate it visually from the curtain or drapery.

Lightweight **fabrics** work well because of the multiple layers. Lining adds body and support to the side hems and heading.

Mount the hardware before you cut to ensure accurate measurements. The curtains can be installed on standard or decorative curtain rods or on pole sets with rings. To hang panels from flat curtain rods, use drapery pins.

Materials

- Conventional curtain rod or pole or decorator rod and rings
- Tools and hardware for installation
- Decorator fabric
- Drapery lining for lined curtains
- Drapery weights for floor-length curtains
- *Buckram*, 4" (10 cm) wide, for pleated draperies
- Drapery hooks

Cutting directions

- The *cut length* of the fabric is equal to the desired *finished length* of the curtain plus the bottom hem allowance (see chart on page 13).

- The *cut width* of the fabric is determined by the length of the curtain rod, including the *returns*, multiplied by the amount of *fullness* desired in the curtain.

- The cut length of the lining is 5" (12.7 cm) shorter than the decorator fabric; the cut width of the lining is the same as the decorator fabric.

- For rod-pocket curtains, the cut length of the valance fabric is equal to the desired finished length from the top of the heading to the lower edge plus the depth of the rod pocket and heading, plus ½" (1.3 cm) for turn-under at the upper edge plus 4" (10 cm) for the hem.

- For styling tape draperies, the cut length of the valance fabric is equal to the desired finished length from the top of the heading to the lower edge plus 5" (12.7 cm).

- For pleated draperies with a 4" (10 cm) heading, the cut length of the valance fabric is equal to the desired finished length from the top of the heading to the lower edge plus 9" (23 cm).

- The cut width of the valance for any style is equal to the *finished width* of the curtain plus 6" (15 cm) for the side hems. If two curtain panels are to be attached to the same valance, base the cut width of the valance on the combined finished width of the panels.

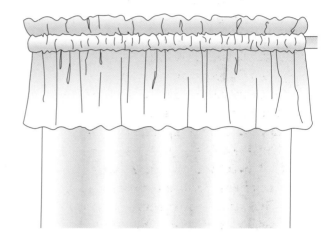

Making unlined rod-pocket curtains with attached valances

1 Seam the fabric widths together, if necessary, for each curtain panel. If half widths are needed, add them at the sides of the panels. Finish the seam allowances together, and press them toward the side of the panel.

2 Press under the lower edge 8" (20.5 cm) for the hem. Then unfold the pressed edge and turn the cut edge back, aligning it to the pressed fold line. Press the outer fold. If the panel has more than one fabric width, tack a drapery weight to the upper layer of fabric at the base of each seam, with the bottom of the weight near the inner fold.

3 Refold the lower edge, forming a 4" (10 cm) double-fold hem, encasing the weights at the seams. Pin. Stitch, using a blindstitch for an invisible hem or a straight stitch for a visible hem.

4 Press under 3" (7.5 cm) on one side. Then unfold the pressed edge and turn the cut edge back, aligning it to the pressed fold line. Press the outer fold. Insert a drapery weight between the layers of the lower hem, and tack it in place. Refold the edge, forming a 1½" (3.8 cm) double-fold side hem. Stitch, using a blindstitch. Repeat for each side of each curtain panel.

 (continued)

5 Repeat steps 1 to 4 for the valance, omitting weights.

6 Press under ½" (1.3 cm) on the upper edge of the valance. Then press under an amount equal to the rod-pocket depth plus the heading depth.

7 Place the valance right side down on a flat surface, and open out the upper fold. Place the curtain panel(s) over the valance, right side down, aligning the upper edge of the curtain to the fold line of the valance. Refold the upper edge of the valance, encasing the upper edge of the curtain. Pin in place.

8 Stitch close to the lower fold through all layers. Stitch again at the depth of the heading, using tape on the bed of the sewing machine as a stitching guide.

9 Insert the rod into the rod pocket and hang the curtains.

Making lined rod-pocket curtains with attached valances

1 Follow steps 1 to 3 for unlined rod-pocket curtains on page 47. Repeat for the lining, but make a 2" (5 cm) double-fold hem in the lining and omit drapery weights.

2 Place the curtain panel and lining panel wrong sides together, matching the raw edges at the sides and upper edge; pin. At the bottom, the lining panel will be 1" (2.5 cm) shorter than the curtain panel. Hem the sides as in step 4, page 109.

3 Complete the curtain as on page 109, steps 5 to 9, handling the decorator fabric and lining as one fabric.

Making styling tape draperies with attached valances

1 Prepare the curtain panels and valance as for the lined or unlined curtains through step 5. Press under 1" (2.5 cm) on the upper edge of the valance. Pin the valance to the drapery panels, as in step 7.

2 Attach styling tape and finish the drapery as in steps 5 to 9 on pages 109 and 110.

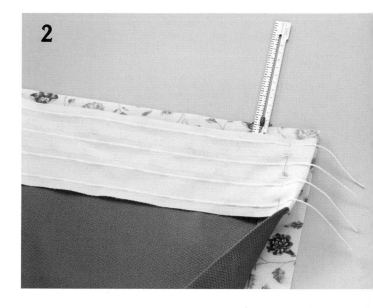

Making pleated draperies with attached valances

1 Prepare the curtain panels and valance as for the lined or unlined curtains through step 5. Press under 1" (2.5 cm) on the upper edge of the valance. Then press under 4" (10 cm).

2 Cut buckram 1" (2.5 cm) shorter than the finished width of the drapery. Tuck the buckram into the upper folds of the valance. Pin the valance and drapery panels together as in step 7 on page 110.

3 Pleat the draperies, using the desired pleat style, following the directions on page 83 or 88 to 93.

111

Tiebacks

GRACEFULLY SWEEPING curves and lavish billows of fabric—features of many impressive window treatments—are held neatly and securely in place by tiebacks. More than a clever mechanism, the tieback is also an integral part of the design and can be made in matching or complementary fabric. Tiebacks can be tailored straight bands of fabric, shallow crescent shapes with welted edges, or even narrow bands with romantic ruffles. They give character and shape to a variety of curtain and drapery styles, from rod pockets to pinch pleats.

Tailored (opposite)
Less is sometimes more. In this window treatment, pleated drapery panels in uniform folds are harnessed with simple tailored tiebacks. Just breaking at the floor, these panels are stationary—only the sheer curtains behind them traverse the rod.

Ruffled (top)
When a little frill won't hurt, a ruffled tieback can be just enough to bring out the feminine side of your curtain. This one is done in contrasting fabrics that stand out against the busy printed fabric of the curtain.

Shaped and welted (left)
Welted, shaped tiebacks hold these large-scale floral panels in perfect proportion to the expansive bay window. The welting repeats the banding fabric, and the rounding off of the tiebacks at the back is a soft touch. The tieback placement is perfectly orchestrated, with slightly higher ones in the back drawing you into the depth of the bay.

What you need to know

Choose a tieback **design** that fits the size and character of your curtain or drapery. Tailored tiebacks can be 2" to 4" (5 to 10 cm) wide. Shaped tiebacks are widest at the center and taper at the rounded ends. For ruffled tiebacks, the band should be in proportion to the ruffle width, usually less than half as wide. The best way to judge the length of the tieback is to wait until you have installed the curtain or drapery and then experiment with a strip of fabric so you know how far you want to pull the treatment back.

Use the same **fabric** as the curtain if you want the tieback to be less noticeable or use a companion fabric to make it more prominent. Stiff interfacing helps the tieback hold its shape against the weight of the curtain. For shaped tiebacks, use a contrasting fabric for the welting to define the graceful curved edge.

Use tieback holders (page 121) and **mount** them at the side of the treatment directly under the *return* of the curtain or drapery. One end of the tieback attaches to the outside of the holder; the other end attaches to the inside. The holder keeps the return edge of the treatment from collapsing against the wall. The general rule for the tieback height is never to cut the window treatment in half. Rather, place the tieback about one-third the distance from the top or bottom of the treatment; often this will be near the sill.

Materials

- Tieback holders
- Tools and hardware for installation
- Paper and pencil for pattern
- Flexible curve or a curved ruler
- Heavyweight fusible interfacing for tailored or shaped tieback
- Decorator fabric
- Fusible web strip for tailored tieback
- Medium-weight fusible interfacing for ruffled tiebacks
- Heavy thread or cord, such as crochet cord, for ruffled tiebacks
- Fusible fleece or interfacing for shaped tiebacks
- Cording for welted, shaped tieback
- Brass or plastic rings or tieback pins, two for each tieback

Cutting directions

- For tailored tiebacks, cut a piece of heavyweight fusible interfacing the finished length and width of the tieback. Cut the fabric 1" (2.5 cm) longer than the finished size. The cut width is twice the finished width plus 1" (2.5 cm).

- For ruffled tiebacks, cut a straight tieback and interfacing as above. Cut fabric for the ruffle the desired width plus 1" (2.5 cm) and two to two-and-one-half times the finished length of the tieback.

- For shaped tiebacks, make the pattern as in steps 1 to 3 on page 116. For each tieback, cut two pieces of decorator fabric and one piece of fusible fleece or interfacing, using the pattern. Cut *bias* strips for welting (page 125) 2" to 3" (5 to 7.5 cm) longer than the circumference of the tieback.

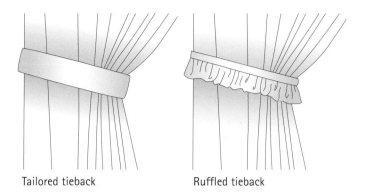

Tailored tieback   Ruffled tieback

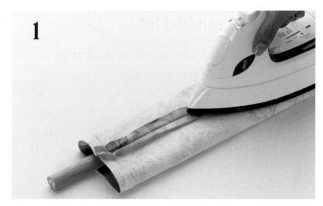

Making tailored tiebacks

1   Press the short ends of the tieback strip under ½" (1.3 cm); unfold. Fold the tieback in half lengthwise, right sides together. Stitch a ½" (1.3 cm) seam, leaving the ends open. Press the seam open without creasing the outer folds.

2   Turn the tieback right side out. Center the seam on the back and press.

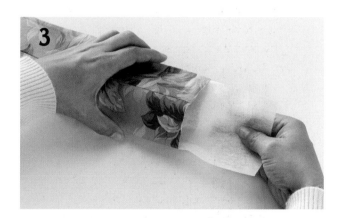

3   Slide the interfacing into the tieback, fusible side toward the back. Turn the pressed ends inside, encasing the ends of the interfacing. Fuse the interfacing in place.

4   Insert a strip of fusible web into each end and fuse the ends closed.

5   Attach a ring or tieback pin to the seam on the back at each end of the tieback. Secure the tiebacks to the holder (page 121).

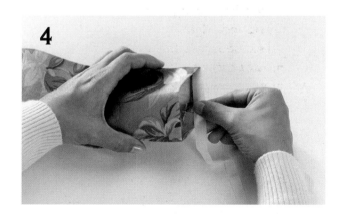

Making ruffled tiebacks

1   Fuse the interfacing to the wrong side of the tieback in the center. Press under ½" (1.3 cm) on one long edge and both ends.

2   Seam the ruffle strips, as necessary. Stitch a ¼" (6 mm) double-fold hem on one long edge and both short ends of the ruffle strips.

(continued)

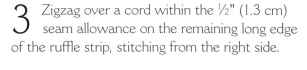

3 Zigzag over a cord within the ½" (1.3 cm) seam allowance on the remaining long edge of the ruffle strip, stitching from the right side.

4 Divide the ruffle strip and tieback into fourths and mark. Pin the ruffle, right side up, to the right side of the tieback, matching marks. Pull up the gathering cord, distributing the fullness evenly. Stitch the ruffle to the tieback ½" (1.3 cm) from the edge.

5 Fold the tieback in half lengthwise, wrong sides together, encasing the raw edges. Pin the folded edge over the ruffle seam.

6 Edgestitch across the ends and along the lower edge if the band. Attach rings to the wrong side of the tieback at the ends. Secure the tiebacks to the holder (page 121).

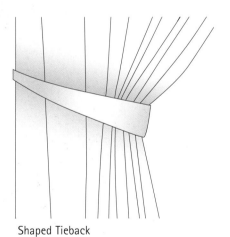

Shaped Tieback

Making shaped tiebacks

1 Draw a rectangle on paper, with the short sides 5" (12.7 cm) and the long sides equal to half the finished length of the tieback. Mark a point on the right short side 3" (7.5 cm) from the lower corner. Mark another point on the bottom line 3" (7.5 cm) from the same corner. Draw a 3" (7.5 cm) line from the first point parallel to the bottom line. Mark a third point on the left short side 2" (5 cm) down from the upper corner.

2 Use a flexible curve or a curved ruler to mark a gradual curve for the upper edge of the tieback, connecting the end of the 3" (7.5 cm) line to the upper left corner. For the lower edge of the tieback, draw a curved line from the third point to the second point.

3 Mark the center fold line for the tieback on the right side. Round the corners on the left end of the pattern. Add ½" (1.3 cm) seam allowances on the upper and lower edges and around the curved end.

4 Cut the fabric and interfacing (page 114). Trim ½" (1.3 cm) from the outer edge of the interfacing. Center the interfacing on the back of the tieback, and fuse it in place.

5 Seam the bias fabric strips together in ¼" (6 mm) seams. Fold the fabric strip over the cording, right side out, matching the raw edges. Using a zipper foot, machine-baste close to the cording.

6 Stitch the welting to the right side of the tieback, matching the raw edges. Start 2" (5 cm) from the end of the welting in an area of the tieback that will be concealed behind the curtain. To ease the welting at the rounded corners, clip into the seam allowances.

7 Stop stitching 2" (5 cm) from the point where the ends of the welting will meet. Cut off one end of the welting so it overlaps the other end by 1" (2.5 cm)

8 Remove the stitching from one end of the welting, and trim the ends of the cording so they just meet.

9 Fold under ½" (1.3 cm) of fabric on the overlapping end. Lap it around the other end, and finish stitching the welting to the tieback.

10 Pin the outer tieback and lining pieces right sides together. Stitch ½" (1.3 cm) from the raw edges, crowding the cording. Leave an opening for turning. Trim the seam allowances. Clip the curved edges; notch the curved of the return end.

11 Turn the tieback right side out and press. Slipstitch the opening closed.

12 Attach a ring or tieback pin to the back at each end of the tieback. Secure the tiebacks to the holder (page 121).

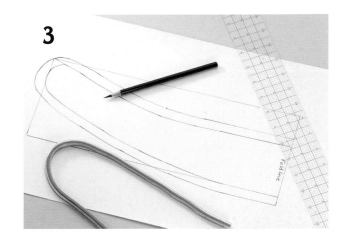

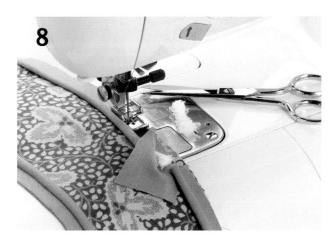

Window Treatment Basics

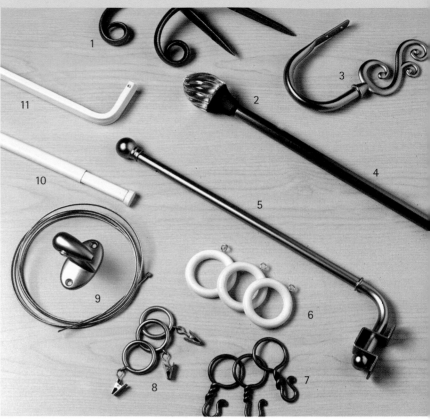

THIS SECTION will help you plan, sew, and install your curtains and draperies. On page 127, you will find definitions of words that are printed in italics.

Choosing and installing hardware

There are lots of choices for window hardware, including multicomponent systems with parts that are sold separately and can be combined to suit any purpose and style. Some items have multiple uses, such as rod brackets (1) that can also be used as holdbacks. Ornate finials (2) can be attached to holdbacks (3) or poles (4). Crane rods (5) are designed to swing away from the window. Wooden and metal rings can be slipped onto a rod and sewn (6) to the curtain, hooked through a buttonhole or grommet (7), or clipped in place (8). A steel cable system (9), used instead of a rod, gives the window treatment a sleek, modern look. When the entire rod will be covered by the treatment, inexpensive utility rods, such as spring pressure rods (10) or oval curtain rods (11) can be used. It is important to install the hardware before measuring for the cut length and width of the treatment.

Where do you mount the hardware? Most curtains and draperies are mounted outside the window frame far enough above and to the sides so the treatment covers the glass and wood. For traversing draperies, the rod should extend far enough to the sides of the window to accommodate the *stacking space* of the pleats. Some styles, like hourglass and stretched curtains that lie close to the glass, are mounted inside the frame on spring pressure rods or onto the frame with sash rods. When the curtains or draperies are layered over another treatment, leave at least 2" (5 cm) of *clearance* between the curtain and the *undertreatment* at the front and sides. If the outer treatment must open and close, leave 3" (7.5 cm) between the layers.

The correct height for mounting curtains and draperies varies with the style, ceiling height, window size, and overall treatment. It should be high enough to cover the top of the window frame or any undertreatments. If you want to create the illusion that the window is taller than it is, the treatment can be mounted higher.

Window treatment hardware comes with mounting brackets, screws or nails, and installation instructions. Use screws alone if installing through drywall or plaster directly into wall studs. When brackets are between wall studs, support the screws for lightweight treatments with plastic anchors in the correct size for the screws. If the brackets must support a heavy treatment, use plastic toggle anchors or molly bolts in the correct size for the wallboard depth. Nails supplied with hardware should be used only for very lightweight treatments installed directly into wood.

Plastic anchors

1. Mark screw locations on the wall. Drill holes for plastic anchors, using a drill bit slightly smaller than the diameter of the anchor. Tap the anchors into the holes, using a hammer.

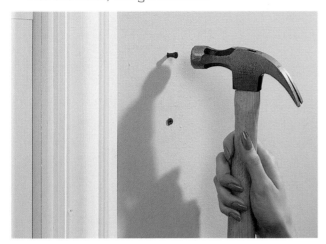

2. Insert a screw through the hole in the bracket and into the installed anchor until it is flush with the wall. Continue to tighten the screw several more turns; the anchor expands in the drywall, preventing it from being pulled out of the wall.

Toggle anchors

1. Mark screw locations on the wall. Drill holes for toggle anchors, using a drill bit slightly smaller than the diameter of the toggle anchor shank.
2. Squeeze the wings of the toggle anchor flat, and push the toggle anchor into the hole; tap it in with a hammer until it is flush with the wall.

3. Insert a screw through the hole in the bracket and into the installed anchor; tighten the screw until it is flush with the wall. The wings spread out and flatten against the back of the drywall.

Molly bolts

1. Mark the screw locations on the wall. Drill holes for the molly bolts, using a drill bit slightly smaller than the diameter of the molly bolt.
2. Tap the molly bolt into the drilled hole, using a hammer; tighten the screw several turns after it is flush with the wall. The molly bolt expands and flattens against the back of the drywall.

3. Remove the screw from the molly bolt; insert the screw through the hole in the bracket and into the installed molly bolt. Screw the bracket securely in place.

Installing a traverse rod

1. Mount the end rod brackets with the U-shaped socket facing upward.

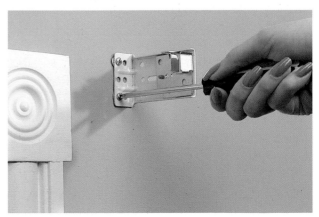

2. Hook the lipped support clip of the center bracket over the center of the rod; position the rod, fitting the ends of the rod into the end brackets. Mark the screw holes for the center bracket.

3. Take the rod down, and mount the center bracket. Lift the rod into position again; snap the center support clip over the rod, hooking it into the groove at the front of the rod. Using a screwdriver, turn the metal cam on the underside of the support clip counterclockwise, locking the clip in place.

4. Push the overlap and underlap master slides to the opposite ends of the rod. At the left side, reach behind the underlap slide for the cord. Pull the cord slightly to form a small loop; hook the loop securely over the plastic finger that projects from the back of the master slide (inset).

5. Separate the stem from the pulley base; hold the base against the wall near the floor, directly below a point 2" (5 cm) in from the right end bracket of the rod. Mark screw locations; mount the bracket.

6. Attach the stem to the pulley base. Pull up on the cord housing, exposing the hole on the inner stem. Insert a small nail through the hole so the stem remains extended. Attach the cord to the pulley, slipping the loop end of the cord through the slot in the cord housing.

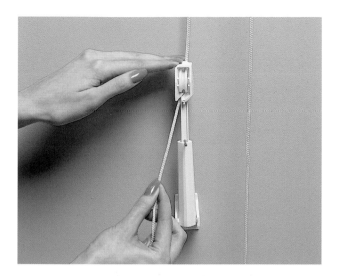

7. Reach behind the overlap master slide at the right end of the rod; locate the two knots at the back of the slide.

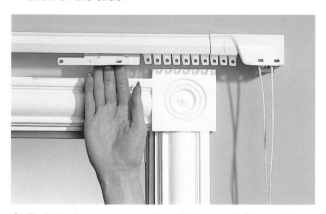

8. Pull the knot nearest the glides until the cord hanging at the side of the rod is taut against the pulley wheel. Tie a new knot in the cord at the back of the slide, with excess cord hanging down. Remove the nail from the inner stem of the pulley. Cut off the excess cord; tighten the knot securely.

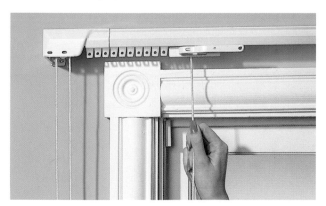

Tieback holders

Short, lightweight curtains with tiebacks can be held in place with cup hooks, small metal tieback hooks, or tenter hooks installed in the side of the window frame or the wall. For curtains and draperies that have more body, however, use plastic tieback holders with a deep projection. These concealed tieback holders are mounted inside the returns at the sides of the treatment to keep the tiebacks from crushing the folds in the fabric.

Mounting boards

Some curtains, such as tent flaps (page 77), are mounted on boards instead of window hardware. The mounting board is covered with extra curtain fabric, much as you would wrap a gift box, but secured with staples instead of tape. Then the curtain is stapled to the board.

The size of the mounting board depends on whether the curtain will be mounted inside or outside the window frame. Stock pine lumber is often the best choice because it is inexpensive, lightweight, and only needs to be cut to the right length. Keep in mind that the actual measurement of stock lumber differs from the nominal measurement. A 1 × 2 board is really $\frac{3}{4}$" × $1\frac{1}{2}$" (2 × 3.8 cm), a 1 × 4 board is $\frac{3}{4}$" × $3\frac{1}{2}$" (2 × 9 cm), a 1 × 6 board is $\frac{3}{4}$" × $5\frac{1}{2}$" (2 × 14 cm), and a 1 × 8 board is $\frac{3}{4}$" × $7\frac{1}{4}$" (2 × 18.7 cm).

For an inside-mounted curtain, the depth of the window frame must be at least $1\frac{1}{2}$" (3.8 cm) to accommodate a 1 × 2 mounting board. Cut the board $\frac{1}{2}$" (1.3 cm) shorter than the inside measurement of the frame so it will still fit after being covered with fabric. Choose the mounting board width for outside-mounted curtains following the general guidelines for clearance on page 118. Install the board to the wall outside and above the window frame using angle irons that are more than one-half the projection of the board. You will need one at each end and others spaced about 36" (91.5 cm) apart.

Measuring the window

For accurate measurements, mount the hardware or mounting board first—don't just estimate where it will be. Use a steel tape measure, not a cloth or plastic one. Measure and record the measurements for each window in the room separately, even if they appear to be the same size.

You'll need to determine the finished length and width of the window treatment before you can figure out how long and wide to cut the fabric. Cutting directions for each project help you do this. If a patterned fabric is used, you will also need to allow extra fabric for matching the pattern (page 123). To find the finished length of the treatment, measure from the rod or mounting board to where you want the lower edge of the window treatment. The measurement is taken from the top of a utility rod or mounting board. When decorative rods are used, the measurement is taken from the pin hole in one of the rings or glides. Depending on the style of the treatment, you may need to add to this measurement an amount for a heading or clearance above the rod. To find the finished width

of the treatment, measure the length of the rod or mounting board. For many treatments it is also necessary to measure the depth of the return. For traversing draperies, you also have to consider stacking space and the center *overlap*. These terms are defined and illustrated on page 128.

Here are some more tips for measuring:

• Allow ½" (1.3 cm) clearance between the bottom of the curtain or drapery and the floor when measuring for floor-length treatments. If the fabric is loosely woven, allow 1" (2.5 cm) clearance because the weight of the treatment will probably stretch the fabric.

• Add 2" to 4" (5 to 10 cm) to the measurement for a floor-length treatment that breaks/brushes on the floor.

• Add 12" to 20" (30.5 to 51 cm) to the measurement for a floor-length treatment that puddles on the floor.

• Allow 4" to 6" (10 to 15 cm) clearance above electric baseboard heaters for safety.

• Short, outside-mounted curtains should fall to ½" (1.3 cm) below the window frame or apron. Treatments mounted inside the frame can stop at the sill.

• If the windows in the room are different heights, measure all treatments in the room to the same height from the floor for a uniform look. Use the highest window in the room as the standard for measuring the others.

• For layered treatments, make underdraperies ½" (1.3 cm) shorter than the overdraperies at the top and bottom, so they will not show.

Working with decorator fabric

Decorator fabrics intended for window treatments have characteristics not found in fashion fabrics. They are more durable and often have been treated to resist stains. When cleaning is necessary, most decorator fabrics must be dry-cleaned to avoid shrinkage. Care information is given on the fabric identification label, found on the bolt or tube.

Decorator fabrics should be preshrunk to ensure they won't shrink during construction or the first time they are cleaned. To do this, roll out the fabric and slowly hover a steam iron back and forth just above the surface. If the treatment is short curtains that you intend to launder, wash and press the fabric before cutting.

To make sure the treatment will hang correctly, the fabric lengths must be cut *on-grain*. Tightly woven fabrics that do not need to be matched at the seams can be cut perpendicular to the *selvages*, using a carpenter's square as a guide for marking the cutting line. For lightweight and loosely woven fabrics, it is better to pull a thread along the *crosswise grain* and cut along the pulled thread.

Seams

Sew your curtain and drapery panels together with ½" (1.3 cm) seam allowances. Straight-stitch seams, sewn on a conventional machine, are suitable for most decorator fabrics that are tightly woven. Seam allowances are usually *finished* together with zigzag stitching or serging and pressed toward the *return* side of the panel. You can also use a 4-thread or 5-thread overlock seam stitched on a serger. Use a very narrow, medium-length zigzag stitch on lace and other loosely woven fabrics to prevent puckering along the seamline. The fabric will stretch slightly as it hangs, and the zigzag stitches can "relax" without breaking.

Before seaming tightly woven fabric, trim away the selvages evenly to prevent the seam from puckering after the treatment is installed. For loosely woven fabrics that would fray easily, don't trim the selvages but clip into them every 2" (5 cm) to allow them to relax.

For sheer treatments that will be seen from both sides, such as stretched and hourglass curtains, join panels with French seams, following these steps:

1. Trim away the selvages evenly.
2. Pin the raw edges wrong sides together. Stitch a scant ¼" (6 mm) seam. Trim the seam allowance edges to remove any fraying ends. Press the seam allowances to one side.
3. Turn the fabric panels right sides together, enclosing the seam allowances. The stitching line should be exactly on the fold. Stitch a ¼" (6 mm)

from the folded edge, enclosing the seam allowances. Press the seam to one side.

Matching patterns

Patterned decorator fabrics are designed to match at the seams. Cuts are made across the fabric, from selvage to selvage, following the *pattern repeat* rather than the fabric grain, so it is very important to purchase fabric that is printed on-grain. The pattern repeat is the lengthwise distance from one distinctive point in the design, such as the tip of a petal in a floral pattern, to the same point in the next repeat of the design. Some patterned fabrics have pattern repeat markings printed on the selvages.

Extra yardage is usually needed so you can match the pattern. After finding the cut length for the main pieces of a curtain or drapery, round this measurement up to the next number divisible by the size of the pattern repeat to determine the revised cut length. To have the design match from one panel to the next, each panel must be cut at exactly the same point of the pattern repeat.

1. Cut the fabric pieces to the revised cut length, allowing extra for matching the print. Place two fabric pieces right sides together, aligning the selvages. Fold back the upper selvage until the pattern matches. Adjust the top layer slightly up or down so the pattern lines up exactly. Press the fold line.

2. Unfold the pressed selvage and pin the layers together, in the fold line. Turn the fabric over and

check the match from the right side. Make any necessary adjustments.

3 Re-pin the fabric so the pins are perpendicular to the fold line; stitch on the fold line. Trim away the selvages, cutting the seam allowances to ½" (1.3 cm). Finish the seam allowances, if necessary.

4. Repeat steps 2 to 4 for all the pieces in the panel. Trim the entire panel to the necessary cut length.

Hems

If you have measured, figured, and cut accurately, your curtains should fit windows perfectly once they are hemmed. For the neatest and easiest hems, follow the procedure used in professional workrooms: sew the lower hems first, the side hems next, and rod pockets and headings last.

Side and lower hems of curtains are always double to provide strength, weight, and stability. The most accurate way to make a double-fold hem is to press the full hem depth under first, and then turn the cut edge under up to the foldline. Cut off the selvages evenly before pressing the side hems.

Curtains hang better when hems are weighted or anchored. Sew drapery weights into the hems at the lower corners and bottoms of seams to keep the curtain from pulling or puckering. Use heavier weights for full-length curtains, lighter weights for lightweight fabrics and shorter curtains. Do not use weights for sheer curtains. They are not necessary for treatments that puddle on the floor.

There are three ways to finish curtain and drapery hems. Test the methods first on your fabric to see which one you prefer.

a. Straight stitch. The stitching will be visible from the right side but is often inconspicuous. This is the best method to use for sheer and semisheer fabrics. Straight stitch on the folded hem edge, using 8 to 10 stitches per inch. Use thread to match a solid color fabric or blend with multicolor fabric. Stitch slowly through the multiple layers.

b. Blindstitch. This is less visible from the right side. Adjust a conventional sewing machine to the blindstitch setting and attach a blindstitch foot. Fold the hem under, leaving the inner fold extending ⅛" (3 mm). Align the guide in the foot to the soft fold. Adjust the stitch width to take a tiny bite into the soft fold.

c. Fusing. This method is quick and easy; recommended for medium-weight, firmly woven fabrics. Fuse paper-backed fusible adhesive strip to the underside of the hem close to the upper edge. Remove the paper backing, and fuse the hem in place. Follow the manufacturer's instructions for fusing. Press from both sides.

Lining

Lining gives curtains and draperies extra body and also protects the fabric from sun fading, supports the side hems and heading, and gives a uniform appearance to the windows from the outside. Lining also reduces light filtration through the treatment, making seams and hems less visible.

Select drapery lining fabric in the same width as the decorator fabric for your project, so that seams will fall in the same location and the finished panels will be the same width. You can choose white or ivory. The best lining is treated for stain and water resistance. For bedrooms, when total darkness is preferred, select blackout lining.

Decorative trims

Welting, fringes, and other decorative accents dramatically change the appearance of window treatments. They give rich style and grace to curtains and draperies by accenting design lines and adding color and textural interest.

Fabric-covered welting

Welting adds an attractive emphasis to seam lines and edges. In a rod-pocket curtain with an extended heading (page 55), for instance, welting defines the upper edge and stiffens it for better shaping. Welting can also be used to accent the outline of shaped tiebacks. Ready-to-sew fabric-covered cording is available in a limited selection of decorator colors and thicknesses.

   You can cover filler cord with the fabric of your choice for a perfect match to your window treatment. To make fabric-covered welting, fabric strips are cut on the *bias* so the welting will be more flexible around curves and corners. Cut bias strips as wide as the circumference of the filler cord plus 1" (2.5 cm).

1. Fold the fabric diagonally so the selvage is parallel to the crosswise grain; cut on the fold. Measuring from this cut edge, cut bias strips of the necessary width, cutting the ends at 45-degree angles on the straight grain.
2. Seam the strips together as necessary; press the seam allowances open. Cut the end of the strip straight across. Center the filler cord on the wrong side of the strip, with the end of the cord 1" (2.5 cm) from the end of the strip. Fold the end of the strip over the cording.
3. Fold the fabric strip around the cording, wrong sides together, matching the raw edges and encasing the cording.

4. Machine-baste close to the cording, using a zipper foot.
5. Stitch the welting to the right side of the curtain, as indicated in the project instructions, matching raw edges and stitching over the basting stitches. Stop stitching 5" (12.7 cm) from where you want the welting to stop.
6. Cut the welting 1" (2.5 cm) beyond the desired end point. Remove the basting stitches from the end of the welting, and cut the cord even with the desired end point.

7. Fold the end of the bias strip over the cord, encasing the cut end. Finish stitching the welting to the curtain fabric.

Twisted cord welting

Twisted cord welting, a stylish alternative to fabric-covered welting, is available in a variety of styles and colors. A welt tape, or lip, is attached to decorative cord for sewing into a seam. From the right side of the welting, the inner edge of the tape in not visible. Be sure to attach the welting with the right side facing out.

1. Pin the welting to the curtain fabric, right sides together, with the cord ½" (1.3 cm) from the raw edge of the fabric and the ends extending 1" (2.5 cm) beyond the starting and stopping points.
2. Remove the stitching from the welting tape for about 1½" (3.8 cm) at the ends.
3. Turn the welting tape into the seam allowance and pin or tape it in place. Turn the untwisted cords into the seam allowance, following the pattern of the twist and flattening them as much as possible.

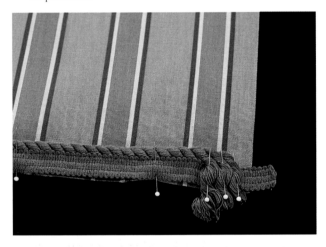

4. Stitch the welting to the fabric ½" (1.3 cm) from the raw edge, using a zipper foot and crowding the cord. Trim the ends of the cord.

Decorator fringes

Fringes come in a wide range of styles and colors, many with coordinating braids and tassels. Fringes that have a decorative heading should be sewn, glued, or fused onto the right side of the curtain. Those that have a plain heading should be sewn into a seam, encasing the heading so only the fringe is exposed.

In the photograph, numbers identify the following types of fringe:

Brush fringe (1) is a dense row of threads all cut to the same length. When you buy it in the store, the cut ends of the threads are secured with a chain stitch, which should be left in until you complete the project. After pulling out the chain stitch, fluff out the fringe by steaming and gentle brushing. Cut fringe has a decorative heading and is similar to brush fringe but not usually as dense. The threads are often multicolored.

Loop fringe (2) is made with a decorative heading. The fringe is a series of overlapping looped threads that can be the same or different lengths.

Tassel fringe (3) is a continuous row of miniature tassels attached to a decorative heading.

Ball fringe (4) is a continuous row of pom-poms hanging from a plain heading. Similar to the popular craft trim, decorator ball fringe is more ornate.

Bullion fringe (5) is a row of twisted cords attached to a decorative heading. Styles vary in length and weight with single-color or multicolored cords. Cotton bullion fringe is casual, while rayon or acetate bullion fringes are very elegant.

Beaded fringes (6) are very chic. They are available in many styles; some resemble cut, loop, or ball fringes but are made with hundreds of beads in all sorts of shapes, sizes, and colors.

Here are some tips for attaching fringe:

- Apply liquid fray preventer liberally to the area of the heading that will be cut; allow it to dry completely before cutting the fringe.
- To attach fringe with a decorative heading, pin or glue-baste the fringe in the desired location on the right side of the finished window treatment, turning under ¾" (2 cm) at the ends of the heading. Straight stitch along the top and bottom of the heading.
- Instead of stitching, fuse the heading to the fabric, using paper-backed fusible adhesive tape.
- Glue the heading in place with fabric glue.

Terms to Know

Bias. Any diagonal line intersecting the lengthwise and crosswise grains of fabric. While woven fabric is very stable on the lengthwise and crosswise grains, it has considerable stretch on the bias.

Buckram. Stiffened fabric that gives support to the headings of pleated draperies. Buckram, available in the decorating department of fabric stores, comes on a roll in a standard width of 4" (10 cm). It is also available, though sometimes harder to find, in 5" and 6" (12.7 and 15 cm) widths for making draperies with deeper headings. You can purchase the length you need. Because cut edges of buckram will not fray, it is also useful for making templates for marking the pleats and spaces.

Clearance. The distance between the back of the rod or treatment and the wall or undertreatment, measured at the front and sides. There must be enough clearance so the layers of the window treatment do not interfere with each other.

Crosswise grain. On woven fabrics, the crosswise grain is perpendicular to the selvages. Fabric has slight "give" in the crosswise grain.

Cut length. The total length at which fabric pieces should be cut for the treatment. It includes allowances for any hems, headings, rod pockets, and ease.

Cut width. The total width the fabric should be cut. If more than one width of fabric is needed, the cut width refers to the entire panel after seams are sewn, including allowances for any side hems.

Finish. To improve the durability of a seam, the raw edges are secured with stitches that prevent them from fraying. This can be done with zigzag stitches that wrap over the edge or with serging.

Finished length. The total length of a treatment after it is sewn.

Finished width. The total width of the treatment after it is sewn, including the depth of the returns.

Flounce. An extra-long heading sewn at the top of a rod-pocket curtain that falls forward over the rod pocket.

Fullness. The finished width of a treatment compared to the length of the rod or mounting board. For example, two times fullness means that the width of the fabric is two times the length of the rod.

Heading. The portion at the top of a rod-pocket treatment that forms a ruffle when the treatment is on the rod. The depth of the heading is the distance from the finished upper edge to the top stitching line for the rod pocket.

Interlining. A layer of fabric encased between the top fabric and the lining to prevent light from shining through or to add body to the treatment.

Lengthwise grain. On woven fabrics, the lengthwise grain runs parallel to the selvages. Fabrics are generally stronger along the lengthwise grain.

Lining. A fabric backing sewn to the face fabric to provide extra body, protection from sunlight, and support for side hems.

Miter. A square corner is made by joining two pieces with a seam at a 45-degree angle.

Mock up. Sometimes it is necessary to make a test curtain to find accurate measurements. Do this by cutting up inexpensive muslin or an old sheet and hanging it from the rod in the same manner you intend to hang the finished treatment.

On-grain. When the lengthwise and crosswise yarns in woven fabric are perfectly perpendicular to each other. If the fabric is not on-grain as it is printed, it will be impossible to match up the pattern or to have a treatment that hangs evenly with straight-cut lower edges.

Overlap. On traversing draperies, the panels lap over each other at the center. The standard overlap distance is 3½" (9 cm).

Pattern repeat. The lengthwise distance from one distinctive point in the fabric pattern, such as the tip of a particular petal in a floral pattern, to the same point in the next pattern design.

Projection. The distance a rod or mounting board stands out from the wall.

Railroading. Normally the lengthwise grain of the fabric runs vertically in a window treatment. Since decorator fabric is usually 54" (137 cm) wide, treatments that are wider than this must have vertical seams joining additional widths of fabric. Railroading means the fabric is turned sideways, so the lengthwise grain runs horizontally. The full width can then be cut in one piece, eliminating the need for any seams.

Return. The portion of the treatment that extends from the end of the rod or mounting board to the wall, blocking the side light and view.

Rod pocket. The fabric tunnel where the curtain rod or pole is inserted. Stitching lines at the top and bottom of the pocket keep the rod or pole in place.

Self-lined. A fabric panel lined to the edge with the same fabric. Rather than cutting two pieces and sewing them together, one double-length piece is cut, folded right sides together, and stitched on the remaining three sides, so one edge will have a fold instead of a seam.

Selvage. The narrow, tightly woven edges of the fabric that do not ravel or fray. These should be cut away on firmly woven fabrics before seaming to prevent pucking of long seams. On loosely woven fabrics, the selvages should not be trimmed off because they are needed for support.

Stacking space. The distance from the sides of the window to the end brackets of the hardware that allows traversing draperies to clear or partially clear the window when the draperies are open. This is sometimes referred to as *stackback*. Roughly estimated at one-third of the total treatment width, this distance must be figured into the finished width of the treatment so you know what size rod to buy.

Undertreatment. A window treatment—curtains, draperies, blinds, or a shade—installed under the top treatment, either inside or outside the window frame. The undertreatment is mounted on its own hardware, independent of the top treatment.